T0015536

10 Steps
to the
Boardroom

10 Steps to the Boardroom

Climb Your Way to Success

G.S. Rattan

PORTFOLIO
PENGUIN

An imprint of Penguin Random House

PORTFOLIO

USA | Canada | UK | Ireland | Australia
New Zealand | India | South Africa | China

Portfolio is part of the Penguin Random House group of companies
whose addresses can be found at global.penguinrandomhouse.com

Published by Penguin Random House India Pvt. Ltd
4th Floor, Capital Tower 1, MG Road,
Gurugram 122 002, Haryana, India

Penguin
Random House
India

First published in Portfolio by Penguin Random House India 2021

ISBN 9780670096091

Typeset in Adobe Garamond Pro by Manipal Technologies Limited, Manipal
Printed at Thomson Press India Ltd, New Delhi

www.penguin.co.in

Dedicated to my wife, Verjeet Rattan,
who stood by my side and created
the path with me, together

To my daughter, Tarunjeet Rattan,
for inspiring and supporting with endless inputs
and giving shape to my dream of writing my first book

Contents

Foreword

There is no shortage of books on management, leadership and on how to build a successful career in a business corporation. Most of these are authored by academic experts who have had very little practical, on-the-job experience. These books contain a lot of concepts and theories insufficiently backed by real practical experience and are lacking in influence and impact, as well as any understanding of the context in which businesses operate and executive careers are built. Mercifully, this book is different.

The author, Gurpal Singh Rattan, is an industry veteran. His forty-eight years of varied experience in teaching, academic administration, manufacturing, quality control and its management, research and development, people management and leadership gives him the credentials to write a book on how to build a successful career in a business corporation in a truly authentic way. In his easy-to-grasp, storytelling way, Gurpal distils years of experience into lessons useful for the reader. His introspective nature makes it natural for him to use his personal experiences as contexts and connect these to well-known management concepts.

In this book, Gurpal talks of the most essential skills and traits needed in an executive to build a high-performing career in a business organization. Qualities and characteristics like the ability to envision the future; empathy and compassion towards people, especially in difficult situations; the ability to handle success and failures with equal poise; self-awareness; humility; the ability and willingness to empower people; the passion to perform; and the desire to learn continuously—are all covered in the book, with anecdotes that Gurpal himself has been personally involved in. He makes a strong case for young executives to choose challenging and tough jobs in the beginning of one's career rather than look for staff jobs that are soft in nature.

Gurpal's book is a compelling one. It is valuable for young, aspiring executives as well as for those who are looking for ways to improve their careers. I wish the readers an enjoyable and rewarding reading and wish my good friend Gurpal great success with this book.

B. Muthuraman,
former vice chairman, Tata Steel

The Start of Your Story

It always starts with a dream!

If the dream is strong enough, it will keep the fire burning within. It can either just be a daydream that you can while away your time with, or it can give you sleepless nights where you burn the midnight oil planning for the future you want. But while we prepare for it, there is that small voice at the back of one's head that keeps you up with the questions: Can I? Can't I?

Say it in any tonality you want, and the result is still the same: anxiety and doubt. While we cannot control the voice, what we can control is how we let it affect us and by how much.

And I am yet to meet a person who has not achieved something—in varying degrees of success—if s/he has set their mind to it. A strong, focused goal is a huge motivator towards planning and aligning one's life journey in an endeavour to achieve it. A clear objective is the basic *mool*-mantra that you need to start this journey. Over the years, you will meet people, acquire knowledge and have experiences that either take you away or towards this goal.

This might not be an easy journey. Especially if you are the first one in your circle to take this step. Your circle of support, in both your personal and professional life, will play a huge role in how you handle each curveball that life throws at you and the speed at which you travel towards your goal. However, the most important factor will always be the intensity of the fire in your belly. Everything else is either a catalyst or a deterrent.

You are the star of the show. This is your movie. The happy ending of this movie called 'Your Career' will have to fight villains and the occasional joker to fight through the climax and reach the top to take the victory lap.

Use this book like a guiding light to achieve your dream of reaching the boardroom, as I did. I will share my journey with you and take you through the steps you must master to achieve THE dream. So, let's get you started!

G.S. Rattan,
the Company Man

1

Setting Expectations

Career Stage: Entry Level

This is the most essential learning at any and every stage of your career. And for you to be delighted with this book, I will also need to set your expectations from it. So here goes . . .

This chapter will deal with the following that you need to know before entering a company:

- **Job Description and Responsibilities**: Know them
- **Area of Jurisdiction**: Toes to step
- **Understand the Definition of Results in the Organization**: Understanding what counts
- **Network and Follow**: Who to network with and where
- **Where to Start**: Find the right department
- **Unique Skill Set**: The game changer
- **Attitude Matters**: Always does
- **Your Plan**

Job Description and Responsibilities

Before you embark on a career in a company, understand the job description that is offered to you. Go through it in and out. Understand the clauses in your offer letter. If there is any confusion or discrepancy, don't hesitate to reach out to the HR manager and recheck. It is their job to clarify your doubts. Do not fear reaching out. This will hold true for every position you transition to.

In the beginning of your career, it is important to understand what the organization expects from you, irrespective of which department you get placed in. Very often, I have seen that at the junior-most rung of the hierarchy, youngsters do not know their responsibilities and the role they are supposed to play in a section. They end up getting bogged down by irrelevant jobs or spending time to keep their immediate boss happy doing sundry activities.

If you know what is expected of you, it will be easier for you to choose and volunteer for assignments. A smart person must know what he has joined the company for and forge a path accordingly, instead of getting stuck at the bottom and doing purposeless jobs. When you have just started out, it is difficult to refuse an assignment point blank from a senior. However, if you already have your hands full with (the right kind) assignments that you need to work on, it will be easier for you to say no and more difficult for them to assign meaningless jobs to you. If you get stuck with a silly job, however, find a subtle way to convey your disliking the assignment which you presume to be of no relevance to add any value.

A lot of companies now have inductions or welcome programmes for new joiners. Don't skip out on them or you might get shortchanged. Having a well-structured training and exposure in goal settings, steps involved to achieve them and knowing what programmes and tools are available for you to achieve your goals is essential. This is not college anymore. No one will share these notes with you and there will be no repeats. After that, your own personal commitment to achieve them and your drive will be essential. No one else can do that for you.

When I transitioned from what was then Metal Box to Tata Steel—with a handful of employees who were chosen to be retained—I was unsure of what to expect. I went about asking and meeting people to understand the company culture. Way back in 1979, there was no Internet to help us gather information. People's network or the grapevine was the only source and often not very reliable.

'Quality Systems' and 'Quality Culture' are buzzwords that a lot of progressive management teams want to instil in their teams. Learn what they mean for the company and how they implement it well in advance. It will help you assimilate faster and hit the ground running. Relevant contributions from you at this stage will get you noticed faster and push you ahead of the pack. While you understand your current job role, don't shy away from asking questions about other job roles. This will help you chart out your course in the company.

Area of Jurisdiction

What can you do and what is off limits? Spend the first couple of weeks observing people and diligently doing your job. Listen to what is being said and what is being communicated. This could mean two different things.

New entrants are often watched keenly in an organization, especially by reporting managers. You can either get very lucky and get a boss who encourages you to contribute and take part or your luck can run out very quickly if you get a boss who views you as an upstart and/or a threat. Both will hamper your progress. Most managers are unable to shed old practices and are very resistant to new ideas, especially when they come from a fresher. They want to play it safe and not upset the cart. This can also be attributed to the overall company culture. It is also true that most mangers do not want to come out of their comfort zone as any new thinking, and its execution, calls for taking up new challenges and putting in a few extra hours of work. That's the place you ought to be in.

I can recall one instance in a previous company where my experience affirmed the above. In this incident, I was reporting to a boss who was resistant to change . . . of any kind.

In a crisis situation, when no previous knowledge helped to resolve it and dependency on a few select troubleshooters was of no use, my suggestion to view it differently was also not acceptable. I approached the company head and briefed him about the new way of looking to solve it. To my surprise, he agreed. I took the situation under my control and resolved the situation to get the perfect results and set an example for others to emulate and start an out-of-the-box thinking process.

When I started out with Tata Bearings on 10 November 1978, for which I ended up working for thirty-two years, I earned invaluable friendships and mentors in my reporting managers: Sudhir Deoras, Harsh Jha and Suren Rao, who welcomed out-of-the-box thinking and encouraged me to push myself. The presence of and meetings with industry stalwarts—like Dr T. Mukherjee, Dr J.J. Irani and B. Muthuraman—always inspired me to put in my best. Some of my career's toughest challenges were thrown at me by these towering personalities to nurture the best in me and help me realize my own strengths.

However, it was not all sweet sailing. I did meet an equal lot who were happy to poke holes and spend hours in inconclusive meetings for any issue.

But now, when I look back, I do notice that because I established a reputation for myself for being an out-of-the-box thinker and was not afraid to voice my views, even at the risk of being ridiculed, I ended up attracting team leaders with similar qualities. But it took me a while to make that known. You are known by the company you keep. Very slowly and steadily, I actively looked to be around and include in my circle friends and professionals who encouraged positive and progressive thinking.

Understand the Definition of Results in the Organization

While you might be keen on putting on your thinking cap every day and contribute to the organization, understand how they define results before going about it. It is easier to first give them what they want and then make a case for what you want to do and explain the benefits. Any successful innovation, improvement or contribution to upgrade the system, however small it may sound, is the first step to getting noticed by the management. It exhibits your inner strengths, your high level of involvement in your job and out-of-the-box thinking that challenges the established Standard Operating Procedure (SOP). When they see results that matter to them, it is easier for them to believe and give you the benefit of the doubt.

I recall, in 1984–85, having made a presentation to improve product quality by keeping a constant *Cutting Coolant* temperature in the most critical machining shop throughout the year to get consistent quality. It was a project taken up under an Annual Quality Improvement Plan. The team of judges comprised of many senior executives and was headed by Dr J.J. Irani, then the president of Tata Steel. After the presentation, the number of questions which were asked by the judges and audiences was overwhelming. I was prepared for all the intricacies involved and got noticed by all. Later on, when we had put up a proposal to the management for funds to upgrade the Central Coolant System, it was not difficult to get it approved.

This success ensured I had 'arrived' at the scene and got noticed by the company's technical experts and decision makers. No frills, no drama, no fanfare: simple plain head work and technical expertise.

It did help that Tata, as an organization, was a pioneer in implementing ISO Quality Systems, JRD QV Management

Systems, and compilation and monitoring of Knowledge Management Index (KMI). They also ensured that they made their employees aware that 'profit' was not a dirty word, but rather the purpose of the business. Though we can choose how we make it. You can choose to better yourself so you leave the competition far behind or you can choose to play dirty and pull each other down. They chose the first method and I am glad they did.

Total quality management across the board and safety were the top-most definitive components of the culture implemented inside and outside the plants along with the implementation of Total Productive Maintenance (TPM). As an organization that felt responsible for its community and other stakeholders, it always looked (and still does) ahead of competition and spent a huge amount of resources to train and impart knowledge to all stakeholders. Team members who embodied these values were noticed and encouraged. I focused on learning and mastering these.

No management worth its salt will stop a young mind that wants to try out something different to improve the system, cut down cycle time to improve productivity and enhance the culture of learning and innovation that creates a lively working environment. Any fresh blood introduced in the system of the organization is meant to think differently and that is the unwritten major expectation from them.

When things don't happen the way the management wants them to happen and a breakthrough is needed, professional consultants are hired at exorbitant costs, putting the bottom line under further strain. But that gives an opportunity for enterprising and ambitious people in the system to add to their learning skills, stay at the forefront, contribute and get noticed. A very high level of zeal and motivation is required to start making your presence felt in the working of the organization. Start on Day 1.

Once you are aware of your target and how it is measured and rewarded, the journey becomes clear and more focused as you will step into your workplace every day with a specific target in mind. This will crystallize your goal; help you master the process and achieve your goal faster. When you enhance your speed on the task at hand, you leave space in your mind to look at more.

Results often don't mean just what is written in black and white in your Key Result Areas (KRAs). These are the tangible results that you can place a tick against after completion. All your peers will be rushing to do the same as well. What will help you stand out is when you learn the intangible results expected of you and start delivering them. This demonstrates perceptive skills that will get your reporting manager on your side. When you start delivering on this, you will quickly move miles ahead of the pack.

Network and Follow

Many organizations have the culture of mentor–mentee in their working system. It's a good move if some senior executive adopts you as his mentee and starts developing you. However, there is nothing stopping you from proactively looking for one within the system. But how do you start?

When we started out way back in 1978, I waited to get to know everyone for a couple of months before seeking out my first mentor, Harsh Jha. The time he took out to speak to me and teach me was invaluable. An incident which made my life easier was taught to me: it had to do with the sharing of knowledge and my expertise with each and every one in the line of working. I reluctantly started doing that and within a few months, I found that the jobs that took too long to get completed were getting done much faster, thus helping the company and giving me lots of time to work on more exciting opportunities. I can still sometimes hear the voice in my head take the form of Mr Jha's voice.

This approach not only gives you moral support and the feeling of being a part of a big organization, but builds up your confidence to face the many challenges you may come across.

However, now we live in the digital era. Things have changed. You can get online and start identifying the professionals who you would like to choose as your mentors. LinkedIn and Twitter are excellent platforms for you to observe them, follow their conversations and engage with them. Based on that, you can decide how you want to move ahead.

What has not changed though is personal interaction. In your first week, take time out to say hello to an individual who you have made an impression on online. A quick, humble hello, a handshake with a smile and genuine words of praise will soften hearts and attitude. It will also speed up your recognition process. However, don't walk in with a sense of entitlement when you meet them with your peers. While you might be a prima donna online, in the company you are still a fresher. Respect experience and designations.

Where to Start

While you can start just about anywhere in a company that you admire, it is always helpful to start your career and stay in line jobs rather than being in staff jobs. Line jobs are basically departments which are always in the limelight and gain maximum attention from leadership teams. Production, Sales and Marketing typically fall into this category and are always watched for their performance. People involved in the functioning of these sections get noticed quickly. If you are a super achiever and want to open the throttle on your career rise, these would be God-sent assignments to show your contributions and get noticed.

Keep learning and enhancing your area of jurisdiction on a continuous basis by demonstrating results, top-notch performance and showing true leadership qualities. Line jobs push you to take independent decisions, think on your feet and own consequences too. In simple terms, they enhance your risk-taking abilities, team leadership skills and mental resilience.

Unique Skill Set

Throughout your life, everyone would have told you to focus on getting good grades. But that is not the game changer.

Everyone who would get into the institute you graduated from or the company you got into would have the same calibre as you. How are you different? What sets you apart? Could it be the Elvis number you can belt or the fiery biryani you can cook up? What gives you your X factor?

While you can choose anything you want, I looked at this strategically. I had limited time in college and was well aware of this. I looked at all the options that would help me create a global career, help me achieve this and make use of an inherent talent that I had. I had an ear for languages, so I narrowed down on learning French. I devoted many of my free college evenings to language classes, much to the amusement of my friends. Incessant teasing followed, but fell on deaf ears. My ears were tuning into French. Notice that I don't use the word 'sacrificed' because I did not consider it as such. This was something I firmly believed would open up more opportunities for me in my professional career. And lo and behold . . . it did!

Attitude Matters

When you start becoming a top performer, you will receive flak from your peers. When you start leaving them behind that hostility might increase.

Your attitude when you perform well will determine how your relationship with your peers goes down. However much you would like to think that you don't need them, you will someday need their support and help or become their team leader. Leading a hostile team is not an easy job.

While you don't need to patronize them or share all your secrets of success, having an easy personality or humble smile helps make it easier. Don't shy away from your success or choose to dim your light because it hurts someone else's eyes, but warn them to wear their sunglasses or learn to be happy for you.

I clearly remember the day when, for the first time, I was picked over the rest of the fresher pack to lead an international assignment to France. While there was one individual who accompanied me, who knew only the technical specs, I was chosen ahead of everyone to accompany them. This did result in a lot of unnecessary friction with my peers, but they could not deny the fact that I was the right person for the job. I was the only person who was good at the job and the only person who knew French. Hours of going to French classes, instead of football, paid off. I became the team lead very quickly. Throughout this, I kept a smile and joked about it. Very soon, the same peers came around and requested me to help them with French.

It reminds me of another incident with our French experts in France, that earned me an interesting epithet. The team wanted to corroborate the results of an innovation done by them to generate the profile on a machined part. The French designer wanted to find out from the Indian team about its working and the type of results we had achieved. When they asked for feedback, no one came forward. Maybe people did not want to upset the French collaborator or were not sure about the issues. Whatever the reason, I felt this was my chance to speak up and probably get answers to an issue I was facing. I was not worried if my seniors or peers thought it was silly. If I had the wrong end of the stick, I wanted to know.

After about a respectful ten minutes, I was the only person who got up from the group, went to his drawing board and wrote about the results and a consistent problem we encountered. They revealed afterwards that this exactly matched the feedback of other French technicians. I even shared how the problem could be corrected. That was the beginning of a strong relationship with the French collaborator, based on equal competency levels which were lacking before. Very fondly, for any technical matter and understanding, the French experts used to advise my other French and Indian colleagues to consult 'The Man with Turban': Me! This good and cordial relationship continued throughout our working and collaborating period.

The top brass feels delighted to get some names of potential leaders during the yearly appraisal time. Apart from performance, they also look for people with the right attitude. This is a key and essential quality for leaders. Good choices on the part of the management reflect that the protocols laid down are working, the chain of command is working, succession plans are working and so are HR policies. It is basically a win-win situation for all to pat their backs and is a great opportunity for an aspiring executive to prepare her/himself and grab the prospective leadership position. But mind you, you won't be the only one in the race. Hence, attitude matters. One can learn a lot here from sportspeople. Sore losers and boastful winners are never appreciated or liked. Graceful losers and humble winners are loved as they display good sportsmanship and strong character.

One of the most influential values of Tata Steel which helped me become an active member of the organization was the humane approach they adopted in dealing with all situations. Especially, and even more so, in extreme critical situations. I have experienced first-hand the company's philosophy in action: stay calm and find a humane solution rather than jumping to a conclusion and taking a decision that might seem obvious.

This value was demonstrated in one of the most critical situations I have been in and left a lasting impression on me. An accidental fire took place at the plant. It was so fierce that firefighters from the local bodies, the nearby Air Force station, and a special team was flown in from Jamshedpur to assist. A particular manufacturing centre was almost reduced to ashes. After the fire was put off and it was time to rebuild the centre, we were all confident that the management would swing into action to find a scapegoat and heads would roll. We all waited for the axe to fall. Hushed discussions around every corner were about who could possibly be pinned for the disaster and who would get the boot. But to the contrary, the Tata Steel management called up all the technical staff and told them to put their houses in order in the shortest possible time. An instant approval for funds was given. All of us were also told to jot down the learnings from this incident so it shouldn't happen again. The message was: don't get further demotivated, keep your cool, get cracking and the management is there to back you up and support you. This is what made the difference. The entire workforce, across designations, pulled together to put the company back.

This is what I call a real humane approach. It made the process of building up—almost from scratch to a full-fledged operating centre in the shortest possible time—a possibility. The time we took to do this also surprised the management. The handling of this situation was a life-long learning for me and many of my colleagues.

Another incident that demonstrated this—not for a day, year or decade, but for the lifetime of every employee—was another disaster. Incidentally, another fire. One that is scorched in my memory. The 3rd of March is a special and joyous day for everyone in the Tata family. It is the birth anniversary of its founder, Jamsetji Tata. Every year, all companies under the Tata family get together in Jamshedpur and hold a parade. On 3 March 1989, I was a part of the Tata Bearings for the parade. While I was still fitting my division with turbans and fluffing it out, we heard a huge cry and loud noises coming from the gallery. I looked outside to see the VIP tent ablaze. My family was supposed to be seated there. All hell broke loose.

In the room where all the team members had assembled and got ready to participate in the parade to pay homage to the founder, a message was flashed to us about the incident. First, there was the deafening silence and then shrieks of panic as we all ran towards the venue. I was praying to God for my family's safety. As the firefighters brought the flames under control, I ran towards the bodies. I still remember going through mangled, burnt bodies, trying to recognize my wife and my daughters. After going through several of those, I looked up through teary eyes to see all of them running towards me. They had been delayed and were, incidentally, responsible for discovering the fire and alerting the authorities about it. When the fire trucks arrived, they stood aside, desperately trying to catch a glimpse of me. We lost almost sixty souls that day and several hundred who were scarred for life. That day is burned in my memory. It could have also been the cause for my leaving the company. For some it was. However, what followed bonded me with them . . . for life.

This was an experience where I was not only a witness, but also a potential casualty. My family and I had escaped death by a whisker. I was in shock. Totally shattered and demoralized, I saw those who were burnt and dead in my nightmares. But gradually, things started settling down. Every day, I am thankful that my family and I are safe.

However, a lot of them were not so lucky. The loss of a child or a spouse and in some cases, both, was unbearable for so many. The Tata Steel management swung into action from the hour of the disaster. With all the resources at their command, the situation was brought under control and the chairman, managing director (MD) and other directors started personally meeting and consoling bereaved families. The best possible treatment was arranged for all the injured, including treatment of burns, plastic surgeries and mental health counselling. While nothing could make up for the loss of lives, the Tata Steel management instituted jobs and scholarships for children, healthcare for the elderly and lifelong treatment for the employee via a special cell to ensure their wellbeing. Everything the management did had a personal touch of genuine sympathy that is so characteristic of Tata culture.

The incident brought up many issues to the forefront: safety and security lapses, emergency escape routes and lack of resources to handle a disaster of this magnitude. A special Fire Injury Treatment wing at Tata Main Hospital, with the world's best facilities, was set up and the affected employees were compensated in kind and many other ways. The whole plan of the big ceremonial parade was redesigned and revisited to avoid similar disasters. The management took the blame on themselves, without pointing fingers at the staff who volunteered to organize this function.

This is what humanity is. This is what being humane means.

You also pick up the same logical thinking and make it a goal of your life, not to deviate from the basic value of treating all humans with kindness. Just because someone else is bad doesn't mean you become bad too. An eye for an eye makes the whole world blind. That does not mean you let them walk all over you. Learn the lesson and move ahead. Be aware and protect yourself, but don't stoop down to their level. This is where you lay the foundation of your team-building expertise and professional values. This pays handsome dividends, not only in terms of your steady growth within the organization, but also in making you calm, cool and sensitive as a person. When crisis hits, organizations want cool heads at the top, not hot heads.

Acquiring the humane approach to dealing with all situations helps all in your line of command and becomes a habit that will benefit you for life. Your colleagues, society, other internal and external stakeholders and your family too become beneficiaries and peace prevails.

Your Plan

The Company You Want to Work in:

Website:

Key Stakeholders:

What I Admire About the Company:

Vision of the Company:

Mission of the Company:

Why I Belong Here:

Job Description and Responsibilities
* JD:
* Responsibilities that I can take on:
* Responsibilities that will require learning on the job:

Area of Jurisdiction
* Performing areas:
* What I can take a shot at:

Defining Results
* Tangible:
* Intangible:

Network and Follow
- Possible Mentor 1:

Network to Follow on
- Possible Mentor 2:

Network to Follow on:

Where to Start:

Department I Would like to Start With
- Option 1:
- Option 2:
- Option 3:

Attitude Matters
- My key strengths:
- What I need to work on:
- What is valued by this organization?

2

Stay Positive and Have Unlimited Patience

Career Stage: Entry Level

- **Adjusting the Attitude**: Positive attitude will sail you through all hardships
- **Consistency**: Success will not be an everyday affair, moments of failure will be aplenty
- **Journal and Record**: Yes, it is important
- **Handling Criticism**: Listening to criticism and rectifying failure will need immense patience
- **Studying Successful Traits**: Creating new habits

The professional world is competitive. No doubt about it. You always need to have an eye out for opportunity and stay ahead of the competition. But how you choose to do it is up to you.

Adjusting the Attitude

A positive attitude will always sail you through all hardships in the competitive world and complex situations. True. But the exhibition of this attitude perhaps needs moderation as per the situation at hand.

To elaborate, you need to stay ahead in the competitive world, but there will be times when you will face failure. You can still keep your chin up, but it is perfectly fine at that point to feel crestfallen and show it. If you are upbeat and positive at this point, then your seniors might think of your attitude as flippant and wasteful. Dig into what went wrong and keep motivating yourself and your team to do better next time but with appropriate tonality.

You need to move ahead. True. You can choose to do it by being unhelpful and pulling down your peers or to move ahead by bettering yourself every day and lend a helping hand now and then. I am a huge supporter and believer of the latter. In all my years as a professional, I have chosen to follow the latter route, however tough it may have been. No doubt there were people who took advantage of this, but in the long run, my way worked. I was called a fool several times for helping lost causes and departments, but I did not give up. I went with smart decisions, but also let those feelings that helped me sleep peacefully at night decide how much and who I should help. I believe what you give is what you get back—multifold. And I am grateful I got help and support in return when I most needed it, because it came back—multifold. Always count your blessings . . . they matter!

Being labelled the team champion or motivator is not such a bad deal. Back it up with relevant ideas and solutions with a touch of positivity and humbleness and you are already ahead of everyone else.

Consistency

Success will not be an everyday affair: moments of failure will be aplenty when you start out. But your performance cannot be affected by these failures. Safeguard your performance from the pitfalls of success and failure. Both take you to extreme ends. While you can use success to enhance performance gradually at a pace you can sustain, safeguard yourself against the dangers of failure. More often than not, it is true when they say that success will have many fathers, but failure is an orphan.

Consistent performance or gradual increase in performance demonstrates that you are mature enough to take failure and success in your stride and can keep a cool head.

When you succeed—show up. When you fail—definitely show up. Share success with your team and dive into discussing possible solutions for failure with equal enthusiasm. Record both to ensure that the lesson is learnt and emulated or avoided, as the case may be.

How you handle failure is a key indicator of your maturity and leadership skills more than success. So, when you fail, do not brush it under the carpet or forget about it. Dust it, shake it, pull it apart and analyse it. Get experts, colleagues and seniors to help you see where you went wrong. Your willingness and zest to learn from the error will not only help you learn more, but also ensure your seniors notice the effort you are taking to rectify it. Have patience with yourself and the system as you solve the unsolvable.

Journal and Record

However boring this sounds, get into the habit of recording your work. Journaling is a great idea. If you do not enjoy recording, take voice notes like doctors or *Star Trek* captains do. This comes in handy not just when you want to introspect or go over a case again, but also during reviews. It requires patience and determination to create records on a consistent basis.

Many well-established organizations with strong HR policies in place give full freedom to individuals to share their achievements at the time of annual performance reviews. It's only the smartest of the guys who can recall whatever they did the whole year. Most of them fail to recall what they did in 365 days, for which they need to be rewarded better than others. Maintaining a record is always handy, so you can face the Performance Review Board—with facts and figures at hand—very confidently. Share your thought process with clarity and how it successfully enabled the organization's growth.

Develop your own format and methodology of keeping track. I personally am very fond of journaling and write most of my notes with a fountain pen in my notebook. But to each their own. Find a process that works for you. Just make sure you are able to pull it up quickly when you need it.

To recount an earlier experience, my first review literally shook me and woke me up. The first time I got an opportunity to fill a self-appraisal form, I couldn't recollect the unique contributions made by me in the year. I wrote a few sentences, thinking my boss knew what I did that year, so I really should not be worried. But that was not the case. In the review, my self-appraisal form looked quite sparse. While the boss recalled incidents here and there, it would have been impossible for him to remember everything, especially when he had to review everyone in the department. I knew I had lost the opportunity. I was not able to articulate my contributions on paper or in person. However, cheated I felt when the results were posted, I knew it was my own fault. A self-awakening took place that year. I vowed to mend my ways and start noting down my contributions and not miss an opportunity when it came knocking again. This was one of the biggest learnings in my initial years. Never make assumptions or take things for granted.

I learnt this the hard way, as no one guided me to do so. But then I shared this with all my team members, asked them to do so and didn't see someone taking credit for someone else's efforts at the end of year. At the time of failure and success, what you need to have is tons of patience to record both events and share it with your team as well. It gives tremendous energy to the whole section when, as a boss, you motivate your colleagues to think and act like you.

Handling Criticism

Listening to criticism and rectifying failure will need immense patience and mental resilience.

Even as your team succeeds and takes the organization ahead, there will be many people readily available to find faults and issue warnings along with letting you know of all the serious implications in the long run, just to scare you. They do their utmost to pollute the minds of the people who matter, but it's your tenacity and logical approach that will take you forward towards success.

I have seen this happening several times over my career spanning forty-eight plus years irrespective of the company. It has more to do with the individual than the organization. If it is a colleague, simply keep your distance. Choose to stay away from negative people. Your inner circle must consist of people who encourage, inspire and are happy for you. The rest of them need to be tuned out. This is essential for your growth, not just in the initial years, but throughout your career. You are known by the company you keep and very soon you start to speak and think like them. Invite and include people in your circle who inspire and challenge you to raise your game.

You will come across a lot of colleagues who—while discussing to find a solution in a crisis situation—will always have a standard answer to all new thoughts. It will vary from 'It won't work, I have already tried it out' and 'I know it' to 'I have been handling this situation or section for the last so many years, don't you dare advise me on how to handle it

this time', and so on. As a smart leader, you need to handle
them with tact and patience, as their skills are still needed by
you, but they have to be convinced about the usefulness of
new ways of working.

This is where your positivity and patience will help you
come out of this tricky situation. And once you taste success,
share the credit with those nagging colleagues. It generally
helps them change their way of thinking and start accepting
you as their helpful and supportive boss.

If it is a senior, it is a little more difficult, especially
if s/he is your line manager. But opportunities do present
themselves for you to prove your worth. Keep an eye out
for them.

At one point, when I was in the Finish Machining
Department, we were amid the peak of a serious crisis in
the manufacturing process. We were heaped with customer
complaints of product failure, with the manufacturing plant
almost coming to a halt. It was, indeed, a serious lapse in the
system and the process owners were pulled up. A permanent
solution had to be found quickly. After a struggle of working
for almost twenty-four hours, the source of the generation
was identified, but the problem persisted. Everyone was
encouraged to suggest solutions. However, any and all
suggestions were torpedoed by specialist critics who were
invited to help us solve this issue.

As luck would have it, these gentlemen colleagues had
to go out of station for an important meeting and they
flashed a message to the top brass about the impending fall in
production and sales without a solution.

But this was a golden opportunity for me and my team members to try out a different way to solve the burning issue. We put our heads together and came up with a solution. I took responsibility for it as a team leader. My team and I took an immense risk and successfully streamlined the process within twelve hours (with the dire warnings of the specialists still ringing in our ears) and brought production levels up to the planned capacity. This not only brought me into the limelight, but also exposed doomsday predictors for their false reports and nagging attitudes. But the incident inspired me to look for many more opportunities all around me, solve problems and keep making my presence felt.

It's not always that all experiments and innovations will succeed. There are bound to be failures. The only thing that brings excellence in your way of working is patience. As impatience is a habit, so is patience. It needs to be developed and one has to work hard not to lose it when it's needed the most. It's a quality lacking in many executives on the fast track to grow in the hierarchy, and that's not a favorable quality to exhibit. I find it very surprising when young executives claim 'impatience' as an honour badge. It is not.

Studying Successful Traits

While you are waiting in the wings to take charge, start identifying leaders from across the world who you admire. Study them. You will often find that there will be a few core values that are common among all of them. That then becomes your go-to bible.

For me, J.R.D. Tata, Akio Morita and Lee Iacocca are the ultimate pinnacles of success. I studied them extensively. The common denominators, that I deduced, of what made them special were calm composure, cool heads, quick decision-taking abilities and long-term thinking and courage to stick to their core values.

A few books that have inspired me immensely are *SMED (Single Minute Exchange of Dies)* by Shigeo Shingo, *Toyota Production System* by Taiichi Ohno and *The Toyota Way* by Jeffrey Liker. I remember B. Muthuraman, the then MD of Tata Steel, gifted one copy of *TPS* to each one of us to study and change our way of thinking. It did. Immensely. I endeavoured then to learn and imbibe them in my daily routines. It was not an easy path to follow.

One of the most essential qualities that I learnt about and strove to imbibe was maintaining a dignified composure in the face of a crisis. It goes a long way in building your team's confidence in you and themselves. I have noticed most successful leaders of Tata Steel had this quality in abundance, and at the most critical situation, it was exhibited in their behaviour and decision-making. And surprisingly, those decisions generally turned out to be the best decisions that helped them come out from under a bad situation and march ahead. This learning not only kept the morals of the team high, but built their confidence in my abilities, leading them to do wonders in their performance.

Thoughts become things. While it is important to keep an eye on the risks, one must always think positive, encourage contributions and acknowledge team effort. When you identify and practice this over and over again, it becomes a habit. And it is possible to create a habit. The 21/90 rule says that if you repeat the same action for twenty-one days, it becomes a habit and if you continue it for ninety days, it becomes a permanent lifestyle change. You become known by it. A positive attitude and unlimited patience are the hallmarks of leaders-in-making on all fronts of life.

Your Plan

Department I Work in:

Current Designation:

Next Promotion (YY):

Next Designation:

Qualities I Need to Reach the Next Level
- Q1:   Identified Mentor:
- Q2:   Identified Mentor:
- Q3:   Identified Mentor:

Journal and Record:

My Preferred Method:

Handling Criticism:

Three Traits I Want to Develop to Manage Criticism
- Trait 1:
- Trait 2:
- Trait 3:

Studying Successful Traits:

Leader 1
- How: Seminar / Book / Movie / Appointment

Leader 2
- How: Seminar / Book / Movie / Mentorship

Leader 3
- How: Seminar / Book / Movie / Personal Meeting

3

Unlearn to Learn

Career Stage: Team Leader

This is that stage of your career where you will get a taste of leadership and yet realize that there is so much more you need to learn:

- **Essentials:** The most important trait and quality
- **Leveraging Past Laurels:** Dos and don'ts
- **Transitioning Roles:** When you become the leader among peers
- **Gaining Depth:** Do not learn the tricks of the trade, learn the trade itself
- **Becoming Indispensable:** You are there to meet company's expectations and goals, not to show off your past performances
- **Your Plan**

Essentials

Learn to unlearn completely, though it is easier said than done. Our education system rewards us for our ability to repeat everything we have memorized with excellence. In life, that does not help. It's good to know the basics, but you cannot let them shackle you to a desk or designation. Learning the rules and then breaking them is how innovation comes about. Very few are able to let go of past learning or suspend them till such a time that their brain can learn something new. Moving out of the comfort zone is never easy.

Think how difficult it would be for you to learn new languages if you were constantly thinking in your own native language and translating it before you speak. Fluency will never be achieved. It is only when you stop your brain from translating and immerse yourself in the new world, that you will be able to make any headway. If you are, however, handcuffed to your learnt skills, you might as well forget about learning new ones.

Whatever stage of your career you are at or designation you occupy, if you want to learn something new, you have to shut that part of your brain that keeps going back to 'how you used to do it' and give the new way of doing things a chance. Imagine how frustrating it would be for your current peers and mentors when you start every discussion with, 'Last year/in my earlier department, we did it like this'. This will be viewed as an ego drive.

You probably got rewarded and promoted because of your past year's success. That has no relevance this year.

What matters is the job at hand and how you excel in that in the current year.

To absorb new inputs in your memory bank, old files need to be deleted and put in a special folder called the Recycle Bin. No, not the trash bin, because you worked hard at gaining this knowledge. You just need to remove it and park it aside for some time, so you have space to assimilate new data and maybe recall new data when required.

Unlearning to learn was one of the toughest things that I learnt in my professional journey and it was not easy. It is a conscious choice that you make every day. This process was expedited when I was pushed out of my comfort zone and the responsibility of turning around a non-performing bottleneck section of the company was thrust on me. I had to learn the intricacies of the new section, new technology and executives and associates, without letting past laurels cloud my judgement.

It indeed called for some midnight oil to be burnt. This incident, though, helped me hone my HR skills. It helped me understand that when faced with a problem involving man and machine, a machine can be fixed with a hammer and tongs, but humans take a nuanced understanding of relationship management to make headway. It is only when I was able to climb over this hill that I started feeling that unique combination of elation and satisfaction at a job well done. It also opened up new doors for me to move ahead. I continued to imbibe this practice of unlearning and learning till I retired. In fact, I still do that. This book is a new path for me. And I intend to pick up a few more skills while putting this together for you.

Leveraging Past Laurels

Dos and don'ts for the effective use of quoting your past laurels and when to stop them is a critical learning. There are always a few key takeaways from experience that stand the stead of time. There is a time to quote your past successes and there are times when you need to listen to others on your team. No one wants you to turn into a meek observer when you get promoted. You got promoted because of certain successes and qualities you would have demonstrated in your earlier role. Retain the qualities that define you, keep the fundamental learning and contribute ideas, keeping in mind the current issue at hand. This has to be done without constantly repeating your past laurels. Let your current success speak for you.

Self-realization of one's own shortcomings is an essential learning, though not one that all of us want to acknowledge . . . at least not easily. One of these is a classic trap of self-glorification which comes in the form of repeat narrations of past success stories. It was once pointed out to me by a true well-wisher that I stop indulging in this practice as I was yet to show results in my current role. In my mind, I was using my past success stories to motivate my team, but it was having an opposite effect on them and making them uncomfortable and irritable.

Learning to set aside my bruised ego to accept this feedback of counterproductive results was difficult for me. I took a day or two to nurse my bruised ego, but then had to decide. Did I want to hold this against my team or take this in my stride and start showing results so that I could show them what success felt like? I decided to change gears and move forward. Over the next several weeks, I worked alongside my team, leading them towards better change. I had to consciously stop myself from talking about past success stories. Biting my tongue to do that was not a pleasant task. But when I started doing this regularly, over a period of time, it became a habit. A natural outcome of this was that I focused more on living in the present and taking actions for a brighter tomorrow.

While I knew what humility was in definition, this incident taught me the valuable lesson of how to have humility, which I encourage all youngsters to have. Celebrate your achievements, but move on to learn more. Don't get stuck with that one Instagram or LinkedIn post. What is next on your plate?

Transitioning Roles

This one is tough. There is no doubt about that. But this will happen many times in your career. You made an entry into the management structure at a certain level and your performance moved you up to the next level. When you move up, you move above your peers and colleagues. While you moved ahead, there will always be many more who did not. While you might be elated about it, there will still be others who will resent you for your success.

Learning to be happy for someone without letting your own happiness mar it is not something that we are taught or rewarded for. Our society rewards us for challenging someone and showing someone up, so being happy for someone else despite one's shortcomings is seen as a sign of weakness. It is, in fact, a sign of maturity and massive strength. I would like to share this with every reader out there. Unlearn spite and learn to embrace happiness for others and yourself.

When you move up the management ladder, while you might be excellent with the technical knowledge you possess, you will not move up after a certain position if you do not know how to handle people. The first test comes when you are promoted above your peers. No decent company will tolerate rifts and commotions caused by bad interpersonal relationships. They seldom take sides. If you choose to take up a high-handed or confrontational approach with your earlier peers, you will run into emotionally charged, turbulent situations. You both run the risk of losing your jobs. If your team does not have your back you might as well be resigned to the current position. You are not going to get any further. So how do you handle them? This will set the tone for all your future promotions.

First, stop complaining.
Don't pass the buck. Don't take it lying down either. A good way of dealing with peers who are now juniors is to set a clean and clear process every time you take over a new position. My go-to method involves having a one-on-one chat with each team member in a friendly setting on my first day. While I would hear them out, I would also lay out a clear vision for the department that I have in mind. Seek their support. Let them

cross question you on the vision and help them understand that you are only looking for team players. Answer every question with patience. A personal approach allows you to deal with diverse individuals with different approaches. Let them understand your vision.

This must be followed by a team meeting that allows all of them to voice their ideas and pool them in to achieve the shared vision.

Second, empower them.

Yes, this is a risky proposition. But you must learn to identify strengths in people and respect them for it. This is where the one-on-one meeting helps. Empower people with certain tasks and acknowledge them for it.

Third, let go of the ego.

It's easier said than done, right? But not impossible. Ego is a deal breaker here. If you let this creep into your relationship with your team, it is building up for disaster. However, keep in mind that there is a difference between self-respect and ego. While you give them space to accept you as a boss, you need to be firm that you will not stand for any disrespect.

Fourth, let go of the guilt.

Winners' guilt is real. I have seen peers who rose above the rest get stifled with guilt and to assuage that, ended up messing their promotions because they wanted to please their friends. How does that help anyone? Some of your peers might quit or ask for a transfer after you get promoted. Let them go.

A fair lot will also stick by your side. These are the people who you need to work with. Here is where your skill set and knowledge will help you establish natural leadership. Be the go-to person!

These are also the people who you need to spend that extra time with—to groom them for their next promotion. This is how you build your tribe, one department at a time.

Gaining Depth

Getting promoted also means new responsibilities and new skill sets that you need to succeed at. There is always a learning curve. The first day, week or month will make you a little nervous and possibly create self-doubt on whether you are cut out for new responsibilities. Every company has a certain amount they dedicate for the 'learning curve'. The sooner you get over it, the better it is for you.

Don't look for short cuts. Roll up your sleeves, get down on the shop floor and learn the trade. Your bosses will appreciate you wanting for learning the trade before recommending changes that rest on past laurels. No department head will say no to your enthusiasm for learning the intricacies of the trade. Very few management-level promotes take the trouble to learn the trade. They do learn it over a period of time. But by the time they do, their peers would have moved on to several positions above them. I have met a lot of people with this disposition in my career. They will ridicule you for wanting to sit with the factory worker and understanding how the machine works, what disrupts the flow and what are the technical aspects that bother them. It's ok. This will pass. Ignore them.

One incident which inspired me to become a strong follower of mastering the technology of your chosen profession was based on the principle of dignity of labour. I, along with a group of officers from our company, happened to visit Auto Expo at Delhi's Pragati Maidan. We had decided to visit the stall put up by a two-wheeler company from China. It was an impressive stall with elegant two-wheelers displayed all over. We observed that there were only two staff members who were managing the entire stall. One of them was working on installing a display bike and readjusting some settings on it. The man had literally rolled up his sleeves and tie and was sweating. After finishing his job, this gentleman met us and introduced himself as the MD of the company. I was surprised to see an MD installing a vehicle and working with his own hands without any inhibitions. I think there could not have been a better demonstration of the principle of mastering craft along with the dignity of labour. The top boss must know the inside and outside of their product and have the confidence and knowledge to demonstrate it, when the time comes to do so. This incident remained with me and became my lifelong motto of never shying away from rolling up my sleeves and getting down on the shop floor to solve an issue.

The 'management' knowledge acquired in colleges is hardly any preparation for delivering results when you have no idea what the floor issue is. At this level, they would expect you to know the 'real' problem. You are the person in the thick of things and should be relied on for practical knowledge and insights. The list is unending. But these five specific skills are a good start and should be at the top of your list:

- Technical: You should be a master at this. Dive into new technical catalogues, technical drawings and specifications you may have not heard, Quality Manuals, SOP folders and customer expectations and complaints. Choose to work with different people in the team who excel at a certain technical aspect of the job and learn from them. Understand how they handle machines and tackle the problems it throws up.

- HR: Yes, this is an important aspect if you want to work within a team and possibly be a bridge between several team members of different temperaments. When you learn something new or a unique way to handle an issue from someone, acknowledge them publicly, give them due credit and thank them. Be generous with gratitude. Never underestimate the importance of good human management. You don't just become the go-to guy because you have technical expertise. You become the go-to guy because people want to work with you. In my career, my closest friends had been HR heads: I used to seek and heed their advice. They study and excel at human relationships. Their advice was invaluable for me.

- Government Regulations: This is a unique skill that will set you apart from the rest. While you grasp the above-mentioned skills and learn them, the understanding of government regulations and their compliance, state and central government laws pertaining to your industry is equally important. This might not be useful right away but will hold you in good stead when you lead the company. A very essential skill when you are at the top. No one will tell you about the faults then. People tend to gloss over their shortcomings and it becomes very difficult for senior management to find holes to plug. Learn when you are in the trenches now. You will know what to set right, what to rectify and what you could possibly throw a spotlight on.

- Volunteer: Find the biggest problem that your seniors are working on in the department and volunteer to help on it. The insight you will gain in the inner workings of the department will be invaluable. Sounds like a no-brainer, right? Surprisingly, it is not. It takes a lot of courage to be on the crisis team, dedicate your time and risk your reputation so early on in your career to solve an issue. It doesn't matter if they only assign you to make copies of documents. Go for it. At this stage in your career, you are at the perfect stage to be a part of the team, share ideas and share the load. What seniors will see is initiative and willingness on your part to be part of a team. A perfect chance for you to showcase your aptitude and positive attitude.

- Become Indispensable: You are there to meet the company's expectations and goals. This expectation and delivery are not set by an imaginary brand, but by your seniors. And the only reason they will give you more responsibility is if you win their trust and let them know they can depend on you. Only when they depend on you can you become indispensable. Otherwise, keep in mind that everyone is dispensable. You are an employee and can be replaced.

This makes me recall an incident in my career wherein I was trying to establish myself in an MNC. I had taken a scheduled break for my annual leave for two weeks. When I got back—I was going through my logbooks and 'IN' tray—I got a call from the VP of the company to meet him immediately. He sounded very agitated. I rushed to find him in a furious mood and cursing all the technical team members who were not able to solve a technical problem of an equipment for the last five days. Due to this error, the production and delivery line had come to a halt, with them finally giving up. The VP wanted me to attend to this issue on priority and rectify it. It sounded like an ultimatum. He wanted me to find a solution. He was in no mood to hear anything otherwise.

A challenge was literally thrown at me. I could have sidestepped the urgency and bought a few days. But I accepted. I rolled up my sleeves and got cracking. I gathered the team that was working on it to understand what exactly was happening and the sequence of incidents. I then gathered my trusted team. We dismantled the equipment to check probable faults and its quality requirements. One by one, with a cool head, we worked on it and finally zeroed in on a few things that could be responsible for the defective output. We worked through the night. We took everything apart and reassembled it and tweaked it, till we started getting the desired output and quality. We operated the machine all night and got the product certified by quality experts. The next morning, it was my turn to contact the VP, invite him to the machine and in the presence of all the stakeholders, show him the product and the accompanying quality documents of the last eight hours. He not only publicly appreciated my work and my team leadership skills, but also showered some of the choicest words on the failing team members. Embarrassing as it was, and I felt for the other team who had been unable to solve it, my heart was pumping with joy at the praise heaped on us. In my mind, I assumed I had reached the group of employees in the 'indispensable' category. But this glory is never permanent and neither is the status.

Learning to get along with people and working alongside them is a key skill that will help you gain their trust. Once you do that, you can count on more responsibilities being added to your repertoire.

In my career, I have seen several times that when senior management gets roadblocked with a challenge, they look for the best guy to take over, irrespective of designation. These moments of crisis are the ones you must identify and turn into challenges for yourself to help you get on the fast track. I have handled several such assignments, gladly many times and reluctantly sometimes. But once you have taken on the responsibility, your only option must be to put your best foot forward and start generating results.

One of the toughest bosses I have served with entrusted me with one of the most badly managed sections of the company. He confided in me that if we were not able to put this back on track, we would have no choice but to shut the company down. This was a huge honour and an even bigger responsibility. Yet, at the same time, I was nervous about the fate of the company resting on my shoulders. I fuelled my courage with all my pent-up nervous energy and dove into the department.

When I took over the department, I defined the mission first and put a timeline to it. I sat down with the entire team, helped them understand the mission and gave them an understanding of how vital the success of our mission was. Without everyone's commitment, it was impossible to achieve this. I only retained those who were committed to the mission in the lead team, irrespective of their designation. The others, I requested to be removed from the department. It was a tough call. Keep in mind that growing up in the management vertical not only requires you to identify the strengths that people bring to the table, but also weed out the naysayers.

Once the core team was set, we identified the problem and gaps, together broke down the mammoth problem into smaller tasks and set up our timelines on what we would do to improve it. The overall timeline was revised every day accordingly.

You recall the HR training I mentioned in the above point? I was the new person on the team. Instead of confronting everyone and getting into arguments, I matched the identified problem with the best person for the job and assigned responsibilities as a team. This was done while ensuring that every person understood that each part of the problem they solved was vital and essential for the success of the mission. I focused on helping them find solutions, identifying further or possible issues and refining the functioning of the department every day.

We kept at the problem with a single-minded focus. Days turned to weeks and months. We put in 12–14-hour workdays discussing the reasons of non-performance, low outputs and frequent quality issues, higher cycle times compared to SOPs and dissatisfied internal and external customers. I motivated everyone by encouraging them to look at this as an opportunity that could rectify the problem and also give us a chance to create innovative solutions. It was a once-in-a-lifetime opportunity for each individual to show their presence and solve the problem with confidence, giving the management no choice but to notice and reward them. It was painstakingly slow at the beginning and it took all my energy to motivate and keep up team morale. But slowly, we made progress each day. Arriving at any milestone was the occasion of celebrations, with a cup of tea and mithai, a typical Indian style of saying 'well done'! A small but very meaningful gesture that did wonders for team morale.

Every morning at 10 a.m., the group would assemble at what I had classified as the 'Quality Corner', where we would do a morning standing huddle. All the information was displayed on a board. This included production figures, quality trends and progress of the assigned tasks with milestones, internal and external customers' requirements and HR issues. A quick review of yesterday's work, priorities set for the day and plans altered, if required. Then everyone would get cracking on the day's job. While I knew I would walk the talk, this approach helped my team members see that in me as well. Every day, I kept a watch on the activities and extended additional resources, which often included me, during the progress of work. I was not averse to skipping my lunch hour and rolling up my sleeves to solve an issue.

Slowly and steadily, results started pouring in. The 'Quality Corner' graphs had started showing remarkable improvement in all the Performance Indices and one day at a team meeting—three months since I took over the problem—we realized we had turned the department around as we had no problems to solve that day. The elation in my team and me was met with surprise, silence and then ecstatic joy! The section which was earlier the bottleneck section for the entire company became a role model for others to emulate.

Many (not all) department heads invited me and my team to give them a briefing on how to handle a crisis, refine the functioning of their departments and become the best. I was happy to share this knowledge with them. I also always ensured that different groups of my team members accompanied me each time so that they also got a good share of the limelight (remember the HR learning?).

I was not shy about sharing these learnings and never held anything back. Some of my peers thought this to be a foolish move as I was apparently giving away the goods. To me, it did not matter. If someone can improve because of the knowledge I have shared with them, so be it. However, what I have learnt will always remain with me. No one can take that away from me. One has got to learn to be confident in one's own experience and knowledge. It is a learnt trait. There will be bouts of insecurities that will creep up on you on an unsuspecting Sunday afternoon. But keep at it. I had to work on it every day and remember that givers gain in the long run. Many people still believe in being grateful and express their gratitude in their own way.

To summarize, approach every task with the zeal of a child and never let the learning spirit die. In the same childlike spirit, remember, playing alone is no fun. You need to learn to make friends and play well with everyone. I was the oldest person at thirty-seven when computers became mandatory in our company in 1984. I was also the oldest person in the management camp when I wanted to learn about new management techniques. I did not shy away from learning and always left the sessions with more knowledge. This same zeal also encouraged me to be the only person, at the age of fifty-four, to apply for Himalaya Base camp with Bachendri Pal, the first Indian woman to conquer Mount Everest. She was the head of the Adventure Club created by the Tata Steel management to encourage all the associates to be bold, adventurous and team players. It was a golden opportunity to learn from a legend. I was not about to let a small thing like age get in my way.

At every learning opportunity—or one that could introduce me to new experiences—I did not care what others thought of me. If I do not learn now, then when? It was a gap in my knowledge and I looked at the first available opportunity to fill it. If you let people around you dictate your learning patterns, you will always move around with half-baked knowledge. And that, as we know, is more dangerous and injurious not only to your health, but that of your team and company at any given point of time.

Your Plan

Current Designation:

Current Department:

Next Designation:

Next Department:

Promotion Timeline:

Essentials
What qualities do I have that will help me excel in my current role?

What qualities do I need to work on/gain to help me excel in my current role?

Who Could Be a Possible Mentor?
Option 1:
Option 2:

Leveraging Past Laurels
Learnings from past department that I must retain:

Leanings from this department that I must gain:

Transitioning Roles

How will I handle peers when promoted?

Qualities I need to have to help me manage erstwhile peers:

Mentor who can help me achieve the above:

Gaining Depth

Three top trade know-hows I must learn in this department

1. .... | Mentor:
2. .... | Mentor:
3. .... | Mentor:

Becoming Indispensable

Below are the notable moments when I became indispensable:

- Case Study 1:
- Case Study 2:
- Case Study 3:

4

Stay in the Limelight

Career Stage: Manager

- **Walk the Talk**: Show results
- **Be Your Team's Biggest Champion**: Do not let personal and team success go unnoticed
- **Handling Negative Colleagues**: There are enough crabs in the organization to pull you down
- **Developing Leadership Skills**: Developing skills that enhance confidence and team management skills
- **Your Plan**

While every phase of your career is crucial, this one is key. It will help you hone your leadership skills and set you on track for a bigger role. This phase should help you become a multi-talented professional who can handle all the curveballs and win the confidence of all the essential stakeholders, establishing you as their preferred brand ambassador, the one who they can trust to represent them at any programme and convince any stakeholder with conviction about the company's good intentions.

Walk the Talk

Produce results. That is imperative. Without this, you are just setting yourself up for a bigger fall. While it is good to talk about your team and your work, if you do not produce results, then nothing else matters. First do the work, put in the time and then talk about it.

I have seen this several times in different stages of my career where individuals start by promoting their abilities suited for the job and making grand gestures and promises with bravado. But when the time comes to actually deliver results, they are all aflutter, and because they have praised themselves so much with respect to their jobs, they tend to back themselves in a corner, making it difficult for them to let go of ego, reach out and ask for help.

In most cases, these individuals start lashing out at their team members or the company, finding fault with people and processes, nitpicking and obsessing about minor details. Not a pretty picture, right? All this in search for an excuse that will help them pin the blame on someone else. How do you think this goes down with the senior management and the team that this individual is working with?

First produce results and then have your game plan ready to amplify the success.

Be Your Team's Biggest Champion

Produce results. And then learn how to showcase them effectively. When you work hard to get results, you should also learn the art of showcasing them. This is a delicate balance between being earnest and boastful, being sincere and overconfident and between celebrating every success and sincere, earned praise that is coveted.

When you burn the midnight oil to achieve the goals you set for yourself and your team, it is human nature to expect acknowledgment by the right set of people. But many times, to your surprise, these compliments and acknowledgments do not reach you in a timely manner. Your immediate senior would have forgotten about it or not noticed the excellence brought to the job by you and your team. It could be possible that they simply forgot, that they did not notice, that they possibly did not know the gravity or the complexity of the issue or that they simply did not want to acknowledge you.

Either way, it brings disappointment your way.

It is often said that expectations beget disappointments. But if you back this expectation with a realistic plan then you can mitigate the risk of disappointments. These slip-ups do take place and are unavoidable. But what was your plan to reduce the risk of omission? My go-to methods involve:

- Talking up my team to my seniors: Never let go of any opportunity—whether it is a dinner, networking event or meeting—to speak well about your team and their individual contributions. I never let go of any opportunity and became my team's biggest champion.

Presenting the team's super stars to the top brass on various recognition forums, allowing them to escort me to explain their successful projects which brought laurels to the organization and introducing them to dignitaries during tea and lunch breaks, showcasing champions and boosting team morale.

- Including the seniors at the right moment: I find this to be particularly effective. Invite your senior at the right moment in a professional environment to praise and acknowledge your team's contributions. This initiative has to be driven by you if you are the team lead. Invite your senior to join you for your next meeting and encourage them to lay praise on your team members. Brief them in advance about each contribution so s/he has the right information to direct praise. Take a step back and let your team be acknowledged and celebrate.

- Bonding with your team: The above always calls for celebrations. While ordering in and sitting in front of the television in a slumber is what passes off as entertainment these days, I am a strong believer in actual human interaction. With every win, my wife and I would put together smaller dinner soirees at our place, giving a homely and personal touch which let the team know they were important to us. These multiple settings encouraged team bonding beyond the office. The comfort level achieved here would often spill over to the workplace, making team functioning more seamless. To these evening gatherings, we would add one or two seniors who we knew would be delighted to hear about our team's developments.

- Coach your team to be team players: Encourage your team to talk about their team's success including theirs. This is crucial. You will always have that one person in the team who would want to take up all the credit without acknowledging that the team makes the dream work. An effective way of countering such damage is to encourage everyone (including this one individual) to speak about the department's success as a team. This includes you. Lead by example and show them how it is done.

- Social media: This is not something I used when I was in this position simply because it did not exist during our time. Now, professionals have an added advantage with social media. I find this tool simply brilliant. Use professional social media networks to talk about your team's success. Make a case study and encourage the company's social media handles to showcase it. Reshare it on your pages by tagging all your team members. Encourage your team members to do the same with their own perspective, adding different narratives to the success story.

- Draw a balance: While there are multiple ways to champion your team and your successes, you have to be mindful about what success you choose to amplify and the path you choose to do the same. If every day becomes a praise session, you run the risk of creating a complacent and overconfident team. The magnitude of the issue or complexity of the problem solved should be directly proportional to the celebration of the success. What requires a kind word? What deserves a public acknowledgement? What needs the boss's attention? When to make a big hullabaloo about it? That decision must be made by you. How you decide to do this will set the bar and determine the kind of achievements your team strives for.

- Take credit: This is essential. While you champion your team, don't let your success and contributions go unnoticed. No doubt this is a difficult balance to draw but you have to put in a word for yourself every now and then so your senior knows who is in command. Temper these self-acknowledgments with humility and kindness.

When you do all of the above, the management will notice how you care about your team, motivate them to be better and encourage an innovative mindset. This demonstrates true leadership and your ability to lead and create a winning team. If you get this noticed, you are primed to move to the next level.

Handling Negative Colleagues

Success is a double-edged sword. It can hurt and reward you with equal precision. As you move up the ladder and gain limelight, there will be a lot of people in the organization who will envy your success. While yes, this is attributed in great degree to human nature, a large part of it is learned behaviour. In our society, we are seldom taught to celebrate the success of our peers. When a child gets a report card from school, most parents will not celebrate their individual success; they will immediately talk about Mr Sharma's son or Ms Sen's daughter who scored more than their own child. The child is subjected to interrogation on why s/he did not score similarly or better. The child learns to hate the success of his/her classmates right there. It takes a strong mind to continue to be happy for their classmates, which I think is unfair of us to expect from a young mind.

This spills over on to the workplace. While this is a discussion that can warrant a whole other chapter, I will stick to the professional workplace. By the time, these children grow up to be adults in the competitive workplace, they seldom learn to celebrate the success of others. While you cannot do anything about all those who exist in the company at this point, because most do not want to learn, start with your team. This is the team that you can mentor and foster to become future leaders, who will create more happy professionals. Start there; it's a good start.

I understand that this seems like an altruistic move and might seem unnecessary to a lot of people. But this is one of the nuggets that will help you change the world. This small team . . . your tribe, will grow with every designation and when you really need champions and positive leaders at a crucial moment to support you. This is the team that will stand with you.

But this does not solve the issue of peers and seniors who would be envious of your success and may also try to take credit for it. This is where you, being the champion of your team, come into play. Own your victories completely. Choose the seniors you involve in the process mindfully, so that they are aware of your success and know whom to credit for it. While you champion your team, your team champions you. When you realize that someone, team or peer, is misappropriating success, you have to put a stop to it immediately. Do not shirk from it. Don't wait for a repeat session. Most people find confrontation distasteful, as do I. But sometimes, these individuals need to be called out or made aware that their behaviour is unacceptable. If unchecked, these individuals will continue to sabotage your career. When things come to a hilt and you do decide to act, it might be too late. Arguing for credit is the worst way to claim it. It sounds like sour grapes and you will end up losing more than you gain.

While peers can be dealt with in this manner, dealing with uncooperative seniors who don't want to acknowledge your success in the fear that you will replace them, is a whole different ball game.

Fourteen years into my career, my department was asked to investigate and rectify a serious product quality issue which needed to be addressed immediately. With consignments being returned and customer complaints piling up, a task force was formed to remedy the situation, failing which bigger orders were at a threat of cancellation leading to huge revenue losses for the company. I led this team with trusted team members. We got cracking and burnt the midnight oil to identify the problem and found a solution. We documented everything, so that it was not repeated. We also successfully implemented it and ensured that both the head of Quality and R&D were in agreement with us. It was a huge win!

We expected huge acknowledgement from our seniors as this literally solved a crucial issue that could have ruined the company's reputation. But we were in for a shock. No recognition. No accolades came our way.

Our immediate boss, who we reported to directly, totally underplayed it. It led to a lot of anguish and dissatisfaction in the team. And there was nothing I could do about it, because I had not anticipated and planned for this. It was a lesson learnt the hard way. When the anger and angst had subsided, I pondered over it to realize that I had not kept the line manager in the loop or shared my success with him. I assumed that since this was a special task force and was led by me, there was no need to keep my reporting manager in the loop. The glory or failure was supposed to be credited to my team and me. But in the actual world, nothing is so cut and dry. Every action has a reaction (equal, appropriate or opposite). A human relationship had been damaged in my enthusiasm to lead a task force with a critical mission. I took this learning to heart and implemented it in my career several times because this was going to repeat itself. You will always find people who expect the credit without putting in the work. However, these people will also have power over your success. How you handle it will determine how much overall credit you can gain in the company.

I understand that a lot of people would say it doesn't matter that the line manager did not feel included. Unfortunately, it does. All it would have taken was for me to have a few conversations with him and keep him in the loop. A relationship that I had nurtured over the years went for a toss because of one incident with him. I had to work overtime to repair it as he was also the person who would be promoting me to the next level.

Twenty years into my career, I thought I had this problem licked. I am reminded of a very important milestone in my career. A new SOP process that my team and I had developed was chosen for company-wide implementation, was a big win for me, and I was excited to share my learning and get the company up to speed. But I was in for a surprise.

We were asked to improve productivity in the Finish Machining section. We worked on various options and it was mandatory to alter the drawings given to us by our collaborator with new specifications for internal and external suppliers. Every decision was based on the customers' feedback and analysis of the customer complaints data. The objective was to have irreversible and permanent change in the system. As a team, we worked for almost six months to conduct Design of Experiments (DOE), get feedback from all stakeholders, meet all the suppliers to study their capabilities in order to meet our stringent quality requirements and how we could help them meet our expectations.

Gradually, we established a new SOP, amended drawings and design, manufactured, introduced new inspection methods in the plant, distributed inspection gauges and methods and advised suppliers to invest in their plants to meet the new standards. The executives and senior employees from other ranks were trained and retrained by me to absorb the new system, and they were sent all over the country to interact with critical suppliers to impart their knowledge and upgrade their systems. They were advised not to leave the suppliers for a few days and initiate the newly designed way of working and issue proper documentation to them and their staff. The whole exercise was to instil confidence in the newly designed system and every parameter which could go wrong was addressed with countermeasures put in place. The implementation was to be in phases so as to not bring the plant to a halt, in case of failure.

As the implementation journey began, I found that in spite of all the care being taken, we were getting mixed results.

It called for a more rigid follow-up and surveillance. It turned out to be a clear-cut case of sabotage by some colleagues and seniors. They refused to support the idea. Some did this bluntly and some in subtle ways. But each of these acts added up to the final tally of implementation of the SOP. Their familiar way of working was being completely demolished and the fact that someone with their own/junior level of experience had put this process together—and hence was not worth considering—could not possibly be better than their way. They would rather see the company fail than see my process succeed. This was a very painful realization for me. It initially baffled me and made me uncomfortable, as I knew most of them very well. Or so I thought. I was hesitant to call them out initially, but as mixed results piled up and we were headed for a possible rollback, I had to decide: Did I like being liked more or did I like ensuring complete success more? I settled on the latter and took up the matter with all of them, addressing their resistance one by one. It was a mighty uncomfortable meeting. But the management stood by my side and encouraged the implementation of the plan. These meetings were never one-on-one. There was always a senior and a junior present with me for the same. This ensured that the happenings and outcome of the meeting was not misrepresented outside the meeting room, especially since we were dealing with an ego issue.

Once we had weeded out the naysayers and set them straight, the results were extremely successful. I learnt quickly that without senior support or the courage to call out people, implementing any idea would not be a cakewalk.

To ensure this did not happen again, finding the right route of information flow was essential. I started a system of getting all line managers briefed by the experts of Quality and R&D regularly. This department was ideal for this task and I chose to drive it from there. This meant that we were there to help everyone improve quality and productivity by giving the 'why' of the changes made and their impact on the final product quality and bottom line. It was our job to help create better solutions and understanding for the overall good, irrespective of the department being addressed. The needs of the many truly outweighed the need of the one in this department without any resentment from anyone.

The objective was to enhance their knowledge and share end-customer feedback that could be leveraged to get a competitive edge in the market. It took off very well. The suggestions and new processes were taken in with a positive attitude. The department also gave us many more opportunities to decimate older ways of doing things and set newer processes that worked well for the entire organization.

Developing Leadership Skills

As life goes on, remember that, as you were once the usurper, very soon you will have someone else walk in with the same gung-ho attitude of changing the world with different, newer and better ideas. It is expected that the new incoming batches will have new techniques and more innovative solutions than the specialist line manager.

It happens every year. Just as you were creating a sweet spot for yourself and finding your stride, along comes a youngster who wants to challenge you. How do you tackle that?

Seeing this youngster as a threat will be against everything you yourself stood for. In my view, you should not be seeing this as a threat but as an opportunity to move on to the next level. If the youngster shows talent, s/he can be trained to take over your job, freeing your time to take on larger challenges. Use the opportunity to move to the next level and learn to refine your leadership skills. Market your department, volunteer for joint projects, lead additional projects with important stakeholders, take an active role in forums, network with the right people, enhance your soft skills, work on your communication skills, enroll in a new course that will help you upskill and enhance your technical skills.

Your new areas of expertise will showcase your ability to take up new challenges. And how you handle them will demonstrate your leadership skills. See how many more things you can look at doing if you have a good team member willing to take the lead? See the advantage.

Our organization was started with collaboration with a French company that wanted to make its presence felt in the automobile sector in India. With a good beginning, things took off well but somewhere down the line, they decided to focus on other markets and lost interest in our region. In the absence of a hand-holding partner and Indian clients asking for a better product compared to other international competitors in the country, we had to decode and understand the complexity of the next generation of products.

I took the initiative of approaching Indian Institute of Technology (IIT), Kharagpur to seek the help of their research scholars and other faculty members; they were to use their expertise to help us upgrade the product quality and process parameters. This idea clicked as the IIT students got the opportunity of a lifetime to work in a manufacturing plant, capture real-life data, analyse it with the help of our experts and identify problem areas where we wanted them to give inputs to improve processes.

Now, this would not have been possible if I did not take the time to identify quick learners and fast trackers in my team and assign responsibility. Work at the manufacturing plant could not suffer while we researched on product quality. I needed team members who I could trust to run things efficiently, while my attention was focused on another project.

And it worked wonders for us as it turned out to be an all-round win-win situation. The IIT faculty started taking interest, along with their research students, and came up with brilliant suggestions to upgrade the product and improvise the process. Engineers like me and others from my team got to work on a project that could change the future of the company. And the young usurpers got a chance to prove their mettle in our absence.

Once that was settled, we dived in. With the commitment and support of the top management, senior members like me, who were leading the team and devoting days together along with our brilliant engineers and the IIT team, made significant improvements in upgrading the product quality.

Soon we involved IIT Guwahati as well to help us in taking up improvements in designing and improvising the process parameters of a special manufacturing and supply module. All this while things back home were running smoothly, thanks to dedicated professionals who wanted to make a mark and got the opportunity to do so.

Today, social media has upped the ante in the workspace. I have seen good professionals ignore it while they are on the job. Me included. I waited till I retired to update my profile. On the other hand, I have also seen visionary leaders and smart young professionals use it while they are on the job. It is admirable how they leverage it to create a circle of influence that extends beyond the job. It stays with them after the job too. Use it while you are on the job. It is your space. No one can take it away from you. My observation tells me that the key here is to be genuine and have something worthwhile to say.

These added skills will help you enhance the senior management's confidence in your profile and position you as an individual who is more suited for a bigger job.

Always be a learner for life. I am still a student at the social media school and every day is interesting. This means that when you take on newer roles, you will fail sometimes. I failed many times before succeeding in getting a Life Cycle Testing (of the products) Rig designed and manufactured as per our requirements. The key was to keep showing up and putting in the time and effort to attain perfection. When we reached a Technical Agreement with Central Mechanical Engineering Research Institute (CSIR-CMERI), Durgapur, on designing and manufacturing a Multi-Bench Test Rig with lots of fanfare and close interaction, we were all excited about it. However, the end product was a total failure. The learning from multiple attempts was crucial and did not go waste. After the agreement came to an end, we soldiered on without them. Multiple failures and unsuccessful attempts gave us invaluable knowledge. We finally created our own testing facility four years later. Persistence paid off. Accepting failure paid off. Learning from failure paid off. Having faith in our own abilities paid off.

As I put this chapter to rest, here's one piece of advice: at this stage in your career know where to put your energies and how to identify people who can mentor you to the next stage. Invest your time wisely.

The major learning was: never give up despite failures and have faith in your own capabilities to fulfil your dream projects.

Your Plan

Career Stage: Manager

Promotion Received:

Next Position:

My Timeline:

Walk the Talk:

Areas I Want to Demonstrate Results In
- Result Area 1:
- Result Area 2:
- Result Area 3:

Be Your Team's Biggest Champion
Ways in which I will showcase my team's success:
Personal
- Method 1:
- Method 2:
- Method 3:

Team
- Method 1:
- Method 2:
- Method 3:

Handling Negative Colleagues:

Ways I Can Handle This Challenge:
- Method 1:
- Method 2:
- Method 3:

Developing Leadership Skills
Five skills I must learn to manage this role and move to the next:
Skill 1
- Method: Self / Mentor / Course:
Skill 2
- Method: Self / Mentor / Course:
Skill 3
- Method: Self / Mentor / Course:
Skill 4
- Method: Self / Mentor / Course:
Skill 5
- Method: Self / Mentor / Course:

5

Focus on Results through Teamwork and Delegation

Career Stage: Team Manager

- **Merging Personal and Professional Goals**: The secret formula to getting both done
- **Secret Ingredient**: The one quality that makes you a natural chosen leader
- **Getting Others on Your Team**: Team members, juniors and seniors start becoming your spokesperson
- **Paying It Forward**: Develop new leaders under you
- **Carry Your Team**: Be the leader
- **Importance of a Succession Plan**: Identify and encourage your successor
- **Your Plan**

Merging Personal and Professional Goals

At this stage in your career, it is a good time to start thinking of where you want to be and how you want to head out. I say this because this particular stage of your career will require consistency and persistence. There will not be many new exciting things that you will get to sink your teeth into. This will, in fact, be the time where you end up giving more and creating teams that require a lot of hand-holding but not a lot of credit. This is the time that you will begin to crystallize where and how you want to grow in your career.

This is also the stage where a lot of people start contemplating new jobs because consistency bores them. Wrong move. This is the time where you know the system well enough to run things smoothly and know it enough to hopefully improve on it. This is also the time you can study the system to be able to plan your future and look for synergies in your personal and professional goals. By now, you know it enough to know who will be able to help you achieve these goals.

If you do decide to move out and into a new job, make sure it is the one you want. At this stage in your career, you are a coveted employee who will break into mid-management and senior management roles easily if you jump. However, this decision is crucial for your long-term prospects, work satisfaction and overall happiness. So, contemplate and weigh the pros and cons carefully before deciding to move ahead.

I say this because I myself had to take a similar decision in my life, when I hit a roadblock in my career growth.

I joined this company fresh out of college and had been with it for five years. As an active team player who contributed enthusiastically to the growth and success of the company, I expected more. More challenges, more influence, more recognition, more pay, more incentives, more upskilling. But there was none. I sensed that this was not coming in any form. The company was not keen on recognizing my contributions or rewarding them. This led to a lot of frustration and anguish in my life and no number of discussions or feelers were cutting ice with the management.

At this point, my career path had begun to take shape and I was eager to get started. The enthusiastic professional in me was raring to go. Dissatisfaction and unhappiness at work were spilling over in my personal life, much to the annoyance of my family. I had to take a good hard look at where I was and where I wanted to be. This was a huge turning point in my career. After multiple discussions with my wife (and yes, your life partner is also essential in this decision if you want to maintain personal and professional harmony) and trusted mentor, I decided to take a huge risk. We weighed what it would cost us versus what we would gain on the personal and professional fronts if we took the risk. We decided to go for it. What helped me make the decision and gave my spouse the confidence to go along with it was my strong belief that this would be a game changer for my life. I had to believe it completely before I could convince someone else.

I put in my resignation and moved to a remote town in another part of the country, taking up a new assignment that would challenge me. Interestingly, the company—

on receiving my resignation letter—offered an immediate promotion with a salary hike and a trip to the collaborators' facilities in Europe and still bigger promises to take care of me in the future as well. And it's a very common trap: stay away from these promises. Leaving an established company, moving out of my comfort zone and uprooting my family to an unfamiliar part of the country was not an easy feat. But the promise of a better life (personal and professional) with a generous salary increment pushed me forward. In hindsight, it was the best decision I took. I dovetailed my personal ambition with my professional one. I knew that whatever the outcome, I would only gain more knowledge and learn from this experience.

If you decide to move at this stage in your career, be very sure that your next job is something you really want. No point in moving from company to company with a pay hike and the same job dissatisfaction. Companies will start recognizing you for what you are and will eventually weed you out of the job race.

Job hoppers who leave the present organization on the slightest pretext must remember the Peter Principle: in a hierarchy, all tend to rise to their level of incompetence, sooner or later.

Over the years, I have encouraged my team to sync professional and personal goals. I realized this is one of the most powerful reasons for one to stay. Every year, I would map out my personal goals and then look for synergies within my professional life that could help me achieve it. Personal and professional goals are intertwined. It would be foolish to think that these can be kept separate. In my role as a team manager and beyond, I have passed on this way of living and mapping out a career to my team members.

Secret Ingredient

There are no secret recipes to meet this goal. Only secret ingredients . . . how you use them will determine your own personal recipe. My wife and I use the same ingredients to make a biryani. Yet, mine is classified as chicken rice and hers as the original biryani; the same ingredients but different results. Both delicious, but each with a different taste. How long you cook it, when you add the ingredients and how you add them makes a huge difference.

Hence, I will share the list of absolutely essential ingredients with you so you can cook up your own recipe for success.

- Teamwork: There is no way around this. You need to learn how to work as a team player. This is where you will either be fast tracked on the management ladder or be pigeonholed into a brilliant consultant, but not management material. Most brilliant executives—with a very high degree of knowledge and impressive skills—fail to grab the top post as they assume that their inherent capabilities will take them to the top. When you are alone and must do the job yourself, a lot of people are brilliant at it because you only have to manage yourself. Issues start cropping up when you must lead a team and have to learn to manage them along with yourself.

- Effective delegation: Easy as it sounds, this is the toughest one. This is one of those non-negotiable ingredients that are crucial to your success. A classic mistake that a first-time team leader does is to assign a task and then micromanage it or remove the person and do it themselves, again and again and again.

  Our company gave us umpteen classroom training sessions, practice sessions and actual hands-on experience with specialists coaching us on delegation as we moved up levels. Finally, we were put back in the workforce after intense training sessions to utilize our newfound skills in the real world. We expected to ace this easily and become masters at delegation in no time. This was easier said than done.

  My department, at that time, needed round-the-clock monitoring. We were given full authority of our departments and were told to get things done. I found that barring a few exceptions, things were not getting done in the allotted time, causing losses and hampering the sequence of operations.

  Every time a problem appeared, I would rush at odd hours in the night, put on my working coat and finish the job myself to avoid embarrassment and humiliation for my team and me. This became more frequent to such an extent that sometimes I was working on a machine alone at odd hours. I was struggling to make sense of why my team was not around and why this kept happening to me. I did everything the seminars taught me and told me to do. But it continued to happen again and again. This was leading to a lot of exasperation between my team and me. Plus, it had started impacting my health.

Two things can come out of this. Either your team figures out that they don't need to do a good job because you will do it yourself anyway or end up either de-motivated or lazy. All outcomes are bad for you and your professional growth. Both will make your team resent you, and you will resent your team.

On one such day, I was sitting alone at the machine while my team was out for lunch. A chance meeting with my mentor helped me see the error of my ways. He sat me down and broke down the issue for me. The issue was me. I was unable to delegate effectively and, in the process, had alienated my team. This was a bitter pill to swallow. But once I had come to terms with the gap in my theory and practical application of effective delegation, I took action. Despite the fact that I had management support, I was unable to delegate because I was simply following rules. I went back to the rule book and started making tweaks to it as per the personality of the team member. Slowly, I identified and took appropriate action on reluctant members of the team.

I realized at this point that the rule book was only a set of rules. Unless you customize it to your situation and team, it will continue to be words on paper and mean nothing to you. For this situation, I modified the rule combination and parameters for each person in my team on an individual level. It worked eventually. But it took a lot of my patience and courage to let my team make mistakes and learn from them. With time, my team crossed the learning curve and honed their skills to my satisfaction and department best standards. Effective delegation requires immense patience and letting others fail without hanging them for it. If you fumble on this one, you will start feeling the heat immediately. When you spot trouble with this, seek a mentor immediately who can help you do this, because it can make or break your career.

- Communication skills: This is one of those non-negotiable social constructs that will help you move ahead. How you communicate, when you do and the tonality you use is as essential as listening to the room, learning how to read between the lines and the person in front of you. This is the skill that will help you push your team's success, talk about your success, communicate your candidature and understanding management with ease. Only one person will get the top job. Being an excellent communicator who is able to get the message across to different stakeholders of the organization is one of the key skills that will push you closer to the next level.

- Building patience: Building patience and learning how to meditate did not come easy to me. I was always a man of action. My advice to anyone who would listen would be to stop wasting time in gossiping, indulging in loose talks at a club, discussing rubbish politics or attending long sessions of meditation or puja. Roll up your sleeves, get your hands dirty and do the work. Work is worship. That is it. Everything else is a waste of time. My wife was of the same opinion.

In 1985, there was a reiki camp held in Tata Bearings. The entire colony of approximately forty officers and their spouses joined in to learn and take advantage of it. The only officer and spouse who did not join was my wife and me. We just could not believe the entire colony had signed up for this.

About a month into the programme, my wife slipped on the stairs and broke one of her floating rib bones. The broken rib could not be put in plaster, and she was asked to go on bed rest. It was very painful for her and very difficult for me to watch her go through it. As a community, we were all supportive of each other, especially in times of sickness and grief. When the neighbours came to visit, within a couple of hours they had organized a schedule. Every day, three times a day, a group of four to five ladies would come over and give her reiki healing. I humoured them and viewed them with scepticism. Slowly, my wife started to get well and would sleep easy without pain medication. I was pleasantly surprised. After she recovered, my wife went on to become a reiki master and so did my youngest daughter. My other two daughters also pursued the course.

No, I did not become a reiki convert, but what impressed me during this entire incident was the calm the practitioners demonstrated in the face of my disbelief. That calm was something worth pursuing. I did my own research and arrived at meditative activity instead of meditation. For me this was a brisk thirty-minute walk every day since then. However late or tired I am, I rarely miss this. When I am on this walk, I don't talk or listen to music. I walk with my thoughts. This helped me spend pent-up energy and use the energy of repetitive motions to fuel my calm. An added benefit was that it improved my health.

- Time management: In any organization, senior leadership's key role is to ensure the team or department delivers on time, be it a product or service. And each organization has a well-defined way to measure the success rate of each assignment. While you know things in depth, without an eye on the timer, your success might as well be counted as failure. Imagine putting in all the ingredients for the biryani, but letting it simmer on low heat for five hours instead of the prescribed one hour on medium heat. When the meal is due in two hours, do you think they will wait for five hours to eat if there is an alternate option available?

- Consistency: Can you deliver results with consistency or are you a flash in the pan? The more you hit the bull's eye, the better you strengthen your case for the coveted top post. On the results parameter, your success cements your position and makes you an undisputed successor to the next level.

Getting Others on Your Team

Finding the right people to be on your team is crucial for its success. This is a crucial skill. You not only have to look at who has the best technical skill for the job at hand, but you also need to think about team dynamics. What combination works so that you can get the best out of your team?

One generally tends to pick people who are like them: classic mistake. Human tendency is to expect others to have the same work ethics and devotion as oneself. Additionally, imagine if everyone in the team is only good at holding the hammer? No one in the team is equipped to hit the nail on the head. A wrong combination and mismatched expectations will lead to frustration. Disappointments set in when there is a (higher or lower) discrepancy here, which generally leads to the leader losing faith in his/her abilities. A lot of people go back into their shell and choose to be exceptional problem solvers or merge themselves into a team where they are asked to do a specific task and not be responsible for larger teams.

It will be equally important to expand beyond the actual team to include supporters or well-wishers of the team, not just for yourself, but also for the growth of the department. Your personal rapport with your peers and seniors and other important members is equally important in setting goals, achievements and acknowledgment. While you manage both these threads, the third thread you need to take cognizance of is managing a watch patrol on the members with crab characteristics and doomsday prophets who might be conspiring against your team's success.

These three threads will have to be woven into a strong rope that will help you move to the next level. This is not a short-term goal, but one that requires fortitude, perseverance and consistency. People will continue to move in and out of your radar. You have to constantly keep helping people evolve along these threads and at every step.

Paying It Forward

The best way to keep growing your team and creating a community of positive leaders is by passing on your learnings. Share your mentor's learnings with them. If you did not have a mentor, then be the mentor you wished you had at that stage in your career. Do this one genuinely. No one is holding you to it. While you will be a mentor to most in your team, identify the person who shows genuine potential. Choose the person you want to help. This might not be a part of your work profile as well. But the more you give, the more you will gain. The immense satisfaction you get from helping others is a crucial piece that keeps you motivated and moving ahead in your career.

A successful mentoring story that I have been proud of was with a colleague who was extremely ambitious and hard working. He would go all out to meet the target with gusto, but when he would get close to the goalpost (which was a sure shot) he would miss the shot. After a few failures in a row, I had a heart-to-heart chat with him. He confided in me that when he saw the target almost being achieved, he would mentally raise the bar to exceed the target set by the management for the department. And then, in order to achieve it, he would start experimenting with the process parameters, which meant he would disregard the SOP and try out some new, unproven parameters to meet his personally modified goal.

During my trip to Annecy, France, in 1982

Strategy session with S.L. Deoras, ex-CEO, Tata Bearings, in 1990

Addressing a Quality Day celebrations function in 1992, along with Harsh Jha, ex-CEO

Visit to Nachi, our Japanese collaborator

Prize distribution to champion colleagues in 2002 at a Performance Excellence through People programme

Receiving Best Supplier award from Bajaj Auto Limited chairman, Rahul Bajaj, in 2005

Explaining some finer points about product quality to MD B. Muthuraman and
Dy MD Dr T. Mukherjee inside Tata Bearings plant in 2006

Welcoming a delegation from a reputed Chinese company in 2006

In my office at Tata Bearings

Verjeet Rattan with B. Muthuraman, MD, Tata Steel, during one of his visits to
Tata Bearings in 2006

Dedicating a club facility to a nearby village as a CSR activity

Trying out stitching after the inauguration of Biplabi Mahila Samiti, Kharagpur, in 2007 (CSR commitments)

TOYOTA KIRLOSKAR MOTOR
TOYOTA KIRLOSKAR AUTO PARTS
9th ANNUAL SUPPLIER CONVENTION

Receiving the Best Supplier award from Toyota India MD in 2007

Receiving certificate of participation for a TQM course conducted by JIPM in Tokyo in 2007

Receiving the JRD QV Merit Certification award
from Ratan Tata, chairman, Tata Sons, in 2008

With Suren Rao, ex-CEO, Tata Bearings

It was a bizarre approach and used to land him in a difficult situation. Then, in his attempt to come back to the proven methodology, he would waste precious time to regain the set output rhythm of the section.

It took me time to counsel and convince him that even if he hits the set target, his rating would be 100 per cent, as he was far ahead of his peers. By choosing to experiment at a crucial juncture, he was setting a bad precedent for his juniors and working staff. I came up with a system and encouraged him to synchronize his working hours with mine especially for the crucial period of the month end or year end. This helped me keep an eye on him and support him through the crucial period. Once he started hitting the goal, he understood and started relishing the pleasure of achieving the set goal in a planned manner, with instant appreciation from team and management. He turned out to be a brilliant asset for the company in the long run.

Our company had a policy of hiring fresh engineering graduates every year to infuse new ideas and energy into the system. Their presence and activities were indeed very appreciable, but most found it tough to make the transition from theory to practice. Our team used to give them enough exposure to help them understand the company's working and its ultimate goal of achieving profit. This covered the entire functioning of the company on a national level, starting from suppliers, production, sales and marketing and end customers.

I decided to take a more hands-on approach with the engineers dedicated to my department. I was heading

Finish Machining, which was unique in its functioning and criticalities. Any mishap or failure would have a catastrophic effect in the whole chain of working. With a fraction of the time spent on theory sessions, I would personally take them to the machines, directly explaining their working principles, salient features and how to monitor critical parameters and their rectification techniques. I encouraged them to roll up their sleeves and understand the machines completely before moving on to understanding the administrative process.

It was imperative they understood that, unless they knew the in-and-out of the machines and were able to solve any problems in them, the rest of the stuff would not matter. At their level, technical knowledge will trump all (see Chapter 1). Keeping my own experience in mind, I knew that if they mastered the technical aspect of the job they were hired to do, the rest could be taught in time. My intention was to help them get over this learning curve quickly and be the mentor I would have wanted at that stage in my career.

While a few thought it was beneath them to sit at the machines and learn, most took it up with zeal and were happy that I took the time to teach them. Needless to say, the former set fell out of the process in a few months and the latter set persevered ahead. With persistence and hand-holding, these young engineers became the strength of the department on whom many responsibilities could be delegated with positive and encouraging results. Their speed of learning was extremely commendable. As we taught them the ropes of the trade with patience and encouraged them to take on more responsibility, each batch turned out to be sincere professionals who went on to climb up the corporate ladder.

As they moved ahead in their career, they were picked up for promotions, international training sessions, attending customer meets and making critical presentations to the top management. Each time a member of my team was picked for a prestigious task, it filled my heart with pride. The grooming of these engineers helped the company in a big way. Watching them do well in life was satisfying enough, but even more satisfying was the fact that it eased out the succession planning and helped me grow as well.

Carry Your Team

You are responsible for your team's success and failures. You carry all of it on your shoulders. No one likes or promotes a person who will take credit for success and dump failures on the team. Giving credit where it is due, identifying the winners and throwing the spotlight on them will not only enhance your credibility in the eyes of your team members, but more so in the eyes of top management. As you move ahead in your career, remember that every year new graduates will come in, new technology will be introduced and new skills will be required to keep moving ahead. Lead your team by being the first person to upskill and learn new technology. When you lead by example, you let them know that life doesn't halt when the rules of the game change. You learn the rules and then change the game. Your team will look towards you to lead them. Their trust in you is what will move you ahead.

Our company had a vision of introducing IT across the board and SAP ERP (Enterprise Resource Planning software) for the ease of managing business. This was announced in 1995 and computers were being introduced in all departments gradually. Many old timers like me were not familiar with computers and the company offered to train middle and senior management executives on the basics of computer learning to start with. Without any inhibitions, I immediately opted for this and started devoting lots of my spare time to upgrading my knowledge, contrary to many seniors who avoided it and delegated this job to their subordinates. The first day of class was a tad intimidating, as I seemed to be the senior-most person there. I braced myself and entered the class with a learning mindset. The trainer was far younger than me and being one of the seniors in class could be perceived as a disadvantage if I were to ask a question. It took me another hour or so to let go of my age prejudice. I knew this was my opportunity to learn. If I hadn't clarified my doubts then, despite the snickering from the backbenchers, I might not have got a chance again. My team members started talking about my newly acquired knowledge and I quickly became at par with them and was able to discuss the subject with ease in person and virtually, I encouraged all my team members to follow suit.

Being a part of the first rush of learners paid handsome dividends as, with the passage of time, I became fairly good at it and could successfully survive the onslaught of the computerization tsunami in the organization that followed. In a couple of years, your proficiency with a computer became one of the parameters that decided how your career progressed. Letting go of my inhibitions, discomfort at being judged for asking questions and learning from young trainers was an advantage that led me far. If I had to, I would do it all over again rather than sitting in a shell and pretending to know.

Carrying a team also means that you will spend a lot of time managing people and planning ahead. If you have the right team working with you, then spend more time micro planning and foreseeing pitfalls, anticipate obstacles and look at providing timely interventions and resources for your team. Your role at the helm will be crucial till the last minute. The game is not over till the last second. A steady and calm hand at the helm is what will result in success.

Importance of a Succession Plan

The easiest route to moving ahead is to ensure that you have a good successor in place. In the absence of a successor, you become irreplaceable and hence unmovable from that department. By refusing to groom a team member or passing on the skill set, you will have dug the hole that no one wants to move you out of and might possibly bury you in. It becomes very difficult for any management to lift the person in the absence of a well-groomed and responsible successor. Many organizations have a very poor succession plan practice, but no one stops you from having this plan ready in your case. As and when an opportunity presents itself, you should be the first person to be considered because you have made plans for a smooth succession. The person whom you are nurturing must have been introduced to the top management and his/her potential acknowledged as a possible successor.

I remember, as a team leader, I would attend several meetings with the top management at various forums in the absence of my company head. These were decision-level meetings that included various performance reviews meetings with the top brass of Tata Steel, review of Quality Systems and progress made on the implementations of various initiatives, business growth proposals with investment details and expected financial impact. I also got a chance to conduct interviews for managerial and non-managerial vacancies along with having a say at management–union meetings at the apex level. Each of these opportunities gave me a chance to gain first-hand knowledge of business complexities.

While on some occasions my senior was genuinely engaged elsewhere, I could easily see that for many others, he would intentionally drop out, pushing me forward. It was an effective strategy. While initially I was nervous for the first few meetings, with my seniors' backing and nudges, I took his absence in my stride and was able to be comfortable in my new role as his representative. It was a risk that he took and I am thankful for it because it paid off. This helped me grow my confidence and explain my perspective on the business. How you present, your hold on the subject matter and the confidence with which you present it, including fielding out-of-syllabus questions with ease at these opportunities will determine your next move.

When I took up the role of Senior Divisional Manger (Plant), I started the practice of getting team managers to present their work to the entire team and management in rotation. Each of them would get a chance to stand up in front of everyone, make a presentation and brief everyone about the monthly performance of their section. While there were some to whom this came naturally, others were held back by stage fright.

I took time out to work with these team managers, review their presentation material and inspire them to have confidence in their abilities. It took a lot of my personal time and dedication. I also made sure this was done in private. I wanted them to take credit for their improvement. Slowly but surely, they improved and, in about a year, I found that there were many enthusiastic and confident executives ready to head the sections and stake their claim to be future leaders. My support, encouragement and effort in pushing them to the next level and throwing a spotlight on them ensured that they were happy to be led by me as well.

Your Plan

Career Stage: Team Manager

Promotion Received:

Next Position:

My Timeline:

Merging Personal and Professional Goals
• Personal Goal 1–Professional Goal 1:
• Personal Goal 2–Professional Goal 2:
• Personal Goal 3–Professional Goal 3:

Secret Ingredients
What I need to work on:
• Skill 1–Mentor:
• Skill 2–Mentor:
• Skill 3–Mentor:

Getting Others on Your Team
Who I want on my team:
• Juniors:
• Peers:
• Seniors:

Paying it Forward

Potential leaders I can mentor:

- Name 1:
- Name 2:
- Name 3:

Importance of a Succession Plan

Potential successors:

- Name 1:
- Name 2:
- Name 3:

6

Learn beyond Your Own Area of Specialization

Career Stage: Senior Team Leader

- **Networking**: Interact with other section heads and senior executives
- **Market Your Team Success**: Share your department's success stories
- **Learn from Successful Leaders in the Company**: Abundant talent and knowledge exist across organizations. Observe, emulate and give due and honest credit
- **Seek Mentorship**: Don't hesitate to ask
- **Your Plan**

Networking

When you work for a long time in a particular section, it puts you in a comfort zone and almost all issues fall in the category of déjà vu. Most just go through the motions. Hence, learning stops and so does growth. Cross learning and horizontal and vertical growth opportunities are also scarce in well-established organizations. At this stage in your career, most of your peers are also aiming for the same position up the corporate ladder as you. They will protect their area of expertise and are rarely tolerant about anyone advising them about it.

I have spoken a lot about networking with seniors in the company and leaders in the industry in earlier chapters. In this one, at this stage in your career, I advise internal networking. The situation as described above can get very uncomfortable. With everyone being guarded, it gets tense in interdepartmental meetings. And God forbid should anything go wrong. The collaborative spirit that a company advocates and has worked hard to inculcate go right out of the window and accusations and finger pointing will be taken to a different level. The spirit of collaboration is in serious jeopardy here. The person who is able to bring these competitive professionals together on the same table and works with the right attitude of getting the job done will be the one who will shine and be the preferred all-rounder. But to be that individual is no easy feat.

Networking with peers is one of the toughest challenges you will face at this point. And the only way you can have any degree of success is by being genuine and authentic. Be sincere in your endeavour to connect with someone. Breaking down the competitive barrier is a gradual task. This can happen over casual meet-ups, family get-togethers or simply in the canteen.

Be a patient listener, good communicator and start socializing. Be genuine and generous with your praise for your peers as well. If you see someone doing something really well, acknowledge it, not just personally but also in public forums. Offer help or advice only when you know the other person will be receptive to it. Seek counsel from an individual who is ready to share his/her learnings. When you find such an individual, return the favour by sharing your learnings. Pick equally genuine people to join your tribe.

Every professional at this stage needs to have a strategy to make inroads in this cross learning. Your personal rapport with your peers and your own networking skills will help smoothen learning across the company and make it easier for you.

Networking takes time and patience. You cannot expect to win over everyone in a single event. You have to work at it. It is often said that you are known by the company you keep. I cannot think of truer words that have been spoken. Your circle of peers, friends and family should encourage, motivate and educate you. Create this circle with a lot of care.

Once you master the art of turning competitors into friends or healthy rivals, you will find your confidence soaring that will carry you through many a promotion.

Market Your Team's Success

Benchmarking is a smart technique that many companies use to learn and bring improvements. This includes studying and analysing the good practices of other successful companies. It is a common technique used to identify areas of improvement and catch up quickly with the progress made by others in the system, process or any other activity. I see no reason why this cannot be applied to an individual.

Your team members, if guided properly, can learn about new ways to operate their work centres, enhance efficiency, and produce better results. As a senior team leader, you should be doing the same for your team.

Inculcate this process in your team. Team leaders working in your department should ideally be a part of the core team that studies benchmarking against other departments and companies along with you. Once you identify the areas of improvement, it is easy to bridge the gap. The success of benchmarking is determined by the severity of the crucial gaps that are identified. And this cannot happen without the pooled resources of your core team.

This is the time to elevate your team to your level and share credit generously. Credit them with success and applaud them. If the work is pathbreaking, then this is the time to enter it into department and/or company awards. Whether you win the award or not, you should be there at that event talking up your team and its efforts in creating an innovative solution. Be genuine in your praise.

Ensure your team is a part of this event. This has a dual impact. Showcasing your team's efforts to your peers and seniors has a positive rub off on your reputation. The team witnessing you showcase their individual and team efforts has a more positive pay off. The sense of camaraderie and bonding that this will instil cannot be created by any other event.

Once your core team tastes the success of innovating and catching up with business competitors, the whole team starts looking forward to creating similar breakthroughs. The credit showered on the team literally works like a magic wand and abundant ideas will flow in to improvise processes and business practices. At this point, you will get overwhelmed with team enthusiasm. This will bolster your team and your team's confidence to a new level. Enjoy the wave of positivity. But here is where you need to be the person with feet firmly on the ground and rooted to reality. You will need to pick the best ideas and be mindful of how you refuse or park ideas for a later date without being condescending or rude.

You are as good as your team's joint strength and success. No one has ever succeeded in turning the corner of their company's future without the backup of an equally competent and motivated team.

Learn from Successful Leaders in the Company

One of the best ways to get acquainted with the complexities of business nuances is by attending all performance review meetings. I know it sounds super boring. Many can't wait to get over with theirs and just go out and party. I am asking a great deal by encouraging you not just to attend yours, but also of other departments and patiently listening. It's a wonderful platform where knowledge is being shared and if one is not receptive to what is being presented, let me assure you, you are missing the bus of a golden opportunity. If you fail or are struggling with peer-to-peer networking, this is the place where you can gain knowledge about all the other departments, their successes and nuances without any concern.

The more interest you take, the more you learn. If you identify areas of improvement, then share them with your peers by first complimenting them on their success and then sharing your possible solution. The tone and manner in which you do this is essential as this favour will be returned and will work to your advantage, if done correctly. When your department review happens, invite a few of your trusted peers to it. Be receptive when others share their feedback. It takes an enormous number of skills, including listening skills and strong observation to grasp what is being shared all around you and make sense of it. But this exercise is worth the effort as these inputs will help you either rise in the organization or help you to survive in the organization. It's a win-win situation.

We used to have monthly performance review meets of each department and I observed that many HODs would skip some of the meets as they felt that the content being shared was of no relevance to them. But I made it a point to sit through all the meets and make my notes on good practices, new initiatives taken and work being done on the HR front to motivate their staff.

But the most exciting meet used to be the one on the Quality Assurance section, where the HOD would share information and feedback from vendors to customers. To many it was boring, but I used to get excited about getting an overall perspective of the business from a service department that was catering to varied customers and stakeholders across segments, helping us revisit many strategies. This, to me, was the ultimate bridge between production and the end customer. And their feedback was valuable. This patient listening and sitting through presentations and discussions turned out to be the most valuable learning of my career. All the inputs from these long discussions gave me great insights for future assignments. I will always stay grateful to my colleagues from these sections, who listened to my queries and sorted out many doubts, helping me understand the subject matter.

The Total Quality Management (TQM) concept was introduced in the company at this point and this department was made responsible for its implementation and monitoring the progress. There was a lot to learn. I always attended these presentations, had started seeking clarifications and offering my sound technical knowledge to clarify many issues with vendors and customers. Initially, I was not taken seriously and felt ridiculed, which was also a method many tried to dissuade me from being part of these presentations. But my persistence paid off. Over time, I was made a part of the Customer and Vendor Assistance Team and started visiting them to listen to their concerns and offer my advice. But I ensured that the solutions offered by me were implemented across the board to make things happen.

Gradually, results started showing and we visibly started making headway. This was rewarded by customers and we shared our success with the top management team. And then came a big change in my career as my role was interchanged with the head of Quality and I was told to implement my successful achievements among all stakeholders. From that point on, I never looked back and kept moving forward.

This gives a golden opportunity to smart executives to enhance the sphere of their knowledge and groom themselves to shoulder higher and broad-based responsibilities with confidence. It also reflects your ability to be a fast learner and a keenness to look for bigger responsibilities. You have to just keep your own fears out of your mind and go after the goal.

These initiatives—taken up by any individual to learn and demonstrate—don't go unnoticed and get acknowledged at the right time and in the right forum.

Seek Mentorship

It is a common folly which many executives suffer from: of not asking for help or seeking out a mentor when learning a new trick of the trade. At a 'senior' position, with seven to eight years of experience under their belts, most think it will reflect poorly on them if they ask for help. They would rather do it wrong or blame it on someone else rather than ask for help. I am often gobsmacked at this attitude.

When you ask for help, irrespective of your designation, you are demonstrating an ability to learn (at any age) and the willingness to get it right. It is a positive trait and not a negative or demeaning one. Learn, pick up the trick and move on.

Ask for help as often as you want. But be mindful about who you are asking for help. You don't want to be known as the helpless boss. I have found that seeking a mentor at every designation helps one confide and talk through concerns. It also helps one learn without fear. Learn and keep making a note of your newly acquired learning.

I took copious notes and put together notebooks at every department. These were with me till the end of my stint at Tata Bearings. I would often pull out the notebooks and refer to them if I could not recall something about a particular problem. Only if my notebooks were not able to solve it would I seek additional counsel.

I often shared these notes with aspiring and ambitious young executives who worked with me. I would advise them to develop the habit of noting down major learnings they thought had enhanced their knowledge and confidence. It only took a few minutes every week. Some followed, some didn't. But after a few years, the gap between a committed professional (knowledgeable, confident and an all-rounder) who continued to work with Tata versus a non-serious professional who slid off the charts was visible. One of my biggest heartwarming moments was when one of these committed professionals acknowledged my advice of making notes on challenges and successes in a review meeting.

It is always beneficial and helpful to have a senior colleague as your mentor to guide you, as and when required. The technique of mentorship is a practical way of learning from the experiences of others without you having to reinvent the wheel. A vast body of experience is available to you in any company. It is up to you to identify who and how to tap for knowledge and leverage it for self-growth and the growth of the company.

When you work with a mentor, go with an attitude of learning. Often, we fall into the trap of showcasing and justifying, instead of really listening to what the mentor wants to teach you. Be open to sharing about the challenges you are facing and listening to the advice being given without being defensive. The advice of a mentor will build your confidence and may possibly prevent you from taking a wrong decision. It will also help you to broaden your social network, which is another fundamental requirement for success. Learn to break virtual and real walls between the knowledge existing in the company and sharing it with the leaders of the future. Namely you, in this case.

Your Plan

Career Stage: Senior Team Manager

Promotion Received:

Next Position:

My Timeline:

Networking
Events I will attend:
- Event 1:
- Event 2:
- Event 3:

Marketing Your Team's Success
Projects I will showcase:
- Project 1:
- Project 2:
- Project 3:

Learning from Leaders
- Leader 1:
- Leader 2:
- Leader 3:

Seek Mentorship
- Mentor 1–Department:
- Mentor 2–Department:
- Mentor 3–Department:

7

Grab Critical and Underperforming Areas and Show Results

Career Stage: Department Head

- **Identify Opportunities**: Look for opportunities across all sections. Grab the critical and underperforming areas
- **Take Up a Challenge**: Identify areas where there have been multiple failures and volunteer to take a shot at them to demonstrate problem-solving skills and a willingness to take up challenges
- **Crowdsource Solutions**: You never know where a brilliant idea is hiding
- **Importance of Risk-Taking**: Your serious and sincere efforts will not go unnoticed, whatever the outcome. If you succeed, you take a quantum jump in your career path. If you do not, then the experience will build your confidence to take up bigger and more rewarding challenges
- **Your Plan**

Identifying Opportunities

This is an exciting phase in your career. You are the lead for the whole department and are solely responsible for giving it direction. Successes and failures are all yours to celebrate, own and learn from.

Among the biggest fears that most professionals at this stage develop is the fear of taking risks along with the fear of failure. They don't want to jeopardize their position in any manner. This pushes them further into their comfort zone and they literally douse the fire in their belly. Asking for a challenge and solving one only when asked are two very different things. Both might have good outcomes, but the attitude is noticeably different. One is seeking to make a change and demonstrates the attitude of a leader and the other is a good little soldier who will solve an issue and demonstrate the attitude of a follower. Nothing wrong in either. But guess where management eyes will rest when they are looking for someone in a leadership position at the next level.

At this position, you have the privilege of being a part of meetings with the top brass. Your enthusiasm got you here. This is no time to curb that enthusiasm and play safe. Attend meetings (however unending they may seem) and listen, to comprehend and understand the bottleneck areas that are hampering the growth of the company. Speak up and volunteer your ideas in these forums. They might not necessarily be issues from your department. Give solutions that look at the big picture and present innovative solutions. Most will not stick their neck out for inter-departmental or other department issues as long as their department doesn't have an issue. Take that risk.

A big company generally faces many problematic areas (for some it's a heap of opportunities). You can choose to focus on any of the problematic areas ranging from current technical issues, investment opportunities, tight time schedules, handling of technological advancements, customer satisfaction, new products, brand image, market leadership, HR, etc. The list is unending, depending on the type of business you are in. Choose to contribute with realistic and grounded solutions to other departments too.

Here is where I would also advise you to let go of the fear of asking other department heads to contribute to a challenge you might be facing. When you contribute with a genuine desire to help (remember all the earlier chapters on networking? The buildup of your reputation will become crucial here), others will follow suit when you are presented with a challenge. And multiple brilliant heads are better than one. Appreciate and thank everyone for their contributions and pick the one that works best for you.

Take Up a Challenge

As a department head you already have seniors, team leaders and teams working for you. While you empower them to get the job done, your time is best utilized by identifying the challenges in your department, troubleshooting, streamlining and increasing efficiency and productivity across the board.

Identify possible areas of growth in your team and set out to solve them. At every department I headed, I would make it a point to set success parameters that were acceptable and set an audacious goal for myself that I would work towards. All team leaders were also encouraged to do the same. As a team, we would look at the efficiency ratio and challenge ourselves to better it.

One of the simplest techniques to find ways to improve and identify non-performing areas is involving local work centre employees. People who are actually working on the machines or are on-ground, interfacing with customers. These are people who are least spoken to in most organizations, whereas they should be the first ones who should be sharing inputs. This could be a management divide, but it ultimately harms the company you are working in. We can sit in boardrooms and dream up apparent challenges, hire highly paid consultants, spend millions on coming up with a solution and then share it with local work centre employees who probably wanted to give a 1+1 free offer to solve the issue.

Identifying the right challenge on which you will focus your energies is a crucial step. Take one up that is worthy of your attention and experience. And if it calls for technological upgradation, introduction of new systems, rotating people to get results or improving the working environment, do it with full enthusiasm. See it till the end. If you put in efforts, you will see results which will build up to give you success.

As a department lead, I would look for the biggest challenge that the department faced and set about solving it. Most often, this had nothing to do with the actual function of the department. It would either be an interdepartmental problem, customer or vendor facing challenge or simply a reputation issue. This would have gone unnoticed because my predecessors would not have thought this to be an important issue worth their time. If the functioning of the department was smooth sailing, I looked for a bigger challenge to solve and bring further improvements.

As part of creating awareness and sensitizing the employees across the organization to learn and understand the requirements of the internal customer, an innovative idea of signing an MoU between two departments was floated. This concept helped one to know about the future requirements of one's succeeding departments and to take corrective action in one's own section to meet those emerging needs. It was just a piece of paper that could remain as such if we so chose to or could be a force to reckon with if enforced correctly. No one would really pull us up on this. I saw the potential of the arrangement and the accountability it brought in. I literally had to force my boss to conduct a quarterly review of the progress made on the set parameters as signed between two HODs.

This concept helped improve the whole chain of manufacturing. Later on, we brought in critical vendors into the fold and encouraged them to follow the system. We added an active element of role-playing during these department meet-ups. We found that all the hardships of training were sorted when the customer and supplier were enacted by the teams. They intrinsically knew the issue but were sometimes unable to see it or refused to see it. The role-play got to the crux of the matter. A lot of times, I would credit it to the individual's zeal to be a better actor trying to best the other. But it worked in the company's favour. This helped both the departments foresee the needs and to meet each other's expectations, and it brought good working knowledge beyond their individual working domain. These MoUs were displayed in each section for all to see and contribute to ensure its fulfilment. We learnt, enhanced knowledge and displayed true teamwork to contribute towards the growth of the company, and in meeting annual plans. It was soon made a part of our KRAs.

I was one of the executives who pursued this concept and brought in new ways of anticipating and planning to meet our targets. The impact was felt across the organization as every member of the section was focused on meeting and exceeding their internal customer's expectations.

Crowdsource Solutions

Each one of us have our own areas of strength and our natural inclination is to help and contribute to sustain the momentum of progress and growth. While there are some challenges that remain with the core team, find enough to share and open it up to the whole department in common meetings.

I have seen in many forums—whenever we have been discussing a serious situation to overcome bottleneck areas—that the most invaluable tip or brilliant advice that saved the day always came from a person totally unrelated and not working in the particular area at all.

In one of the most bottlenecked departments I was heading, output continued to decline without any significant improvement and the management had a very serious view on the prevailing situation. Many technical solutions were tried out, but the output was not able to keep pace with the succeeding section. I, being the HOD of that section, was always under pressure to deliver and catch up with others. As a part of my routine discussions with my supplier department—when we were reviewing drawings and various other specifications—we started to question why one of the quality parameters was so stringent and thus causing a slowdown in output of subsequent operations, and if it really made any impact on quality parameters. During one of these review meetings, one of the young engineers from the supplier department—who was representing the HOD in his absence—brought data for the previous three years and showed that this particular parameter had nil impact on the quality of subsequent operations of the process.

This triggered a cascading thought process and we amended the drawings on a trial basis and conducted the trials by taking all in confidence. There was no dearth of doomsday predictors on this trial. But lo behold, it worked fantastically well (Remember the 5-Why, 1-How technique: It always works only if we follow it systematically).

Once this bottleneck machining centre was brought under control and raised the output to almost 100 per cent efficiency, the rest of the subsequent operations also caught up. All the shortfalls of supply to the internal customer were fulfilled beyond their expectations, which brought us tremendous appreciation from the top management and enhanced the customer satisfaction levels of many external customers as well. This breakthrough and the approach brought me in the limelight and within a year's time, I was elevated to the next senior position as Head of the Plant.

This also taught me that while having quality parameters is fine, they have to be rooted in reality and tweaked to the industry you are in (Genchi Genbutsu: Toyota's mantra of '*Go to the source to find the facts to make correct decisions, build consensus and achieve goals at the best speed*'). Mindless piling up of parameters not only stresses out the people trying to live up to their expectations, but also hampers the overall functioning of the company. Instead of being the lubricant that ensures smooth functioning of the machine, it becomes a spanner in the works, bringing things to a standstill. Once things are functioning smoothly, look for ways to refine that process to bring in perfection without hampering the actual process.

It also showed me that distance also gives a fresh perspective. Here is where you also have the opportunity to train your team to appreciate brilliant advice and give credit, irrespective of the designation of the individual. It will require a lot of tact from you to be able to demonstrate that and set an example without hurting the sentiments of the stalwarts in your team. Each one of us has a brilliant idea tucked away in their minds and is capable of contribution.

But here also lies another big opportunity for you to crowdsource these brilliant ideas and put together a plan that is pathbreaking.

Each opportunity is a big challenge for everyone in the organization and to exhibit your attitude and keenness to solve it. I recall that once, a suggestion given by an employee from the maintenance department for grinding section, to find a permanent solution to improve the performance of a group of machining centres, was very sportingly accepted by the section head. And the performance not only improved, yielding more consistent output, but also brought down recurring costs, culminating in faster career growth of the section head as well as the person whose idea was implemented.

In our personal lives too, we come across many challenges and try to conquer them to move towards happy and peaceful living. Without any challenge, life becomes monotonous and complacent, and one loses purpose in life. So, professional challenges are always a welcome development in the growth of a person's career. They will keep you sharp and motivated.

Importance of Risk-Taking

We often find that when a particular big section or division is not working to its full potential, most executives don't want to touch it with a bargepole for fear of tarnishing their track records.

Any executive taking the responsibility to mend it voluntarily is pretty much jumping into the frying pan and is mentally ready for his/her obituary. Not to mention the nudges and winks; that you see in the room for the professional quickly labelled as 'too ambitious for his/her own good' or 'over-enthusiastic'. But then . . . no pain no gain, right?

Imagine a scenario where the whole chain of management is readily extending unfiltered support to you to ensure you succeed. When would you find such a scenario building up for you, sans a crisis? This is the highest level of motivation. And trust me, a determined individual with a plan can do a lot more than an intelligent one without motivation or a plan.

In my career, I got a lot of opportunities to put many sections or a corner of an important section on the right track, to the delight of the concerned manager. The first one was tough for me as I proposed a cost-cutting measure in the section of a peer manager. I have to admit it was not an easy task. It was a little scary to literally trespass in another territory, and both my personal and professional friendship with that individual was at risk. But then the idiom 'No Risk, No Gain' was playing at the back of my mind. I suggested the idea and let them know it was coming from a place of genuine concern and a willingness to help. The concerned manager and team knew my track record and gained the confidence to risk implementing the suggestion. I explained the technical features and helped them understand that it was a no-risk scenario for them and would not impact the final product, even if the trial failed. All agreed and it became a successful trial and the concerned manager, a very mature professional, thanked me profusely for it. Because of my intervention, he could keep his process cost under check and meet his targets. But it gave me tremendous confidence that one must keep looking for these opportunities beyond their own area of specialization and make an impact.

That was the first step. But from then on, there was no looking back. I steadily became the go-to person for any problem-solving or crisis management in any department and was often consulted on a wide variety of issues across verticals.

It could only be achieved by providing exemplary support to the team with advice, inputs and sometimes just a patient ear. The secret: absolutely no hesitation in discussing the new way with everyone in the section. The secret sauce: tonality and attitude. How you put forward your suggestion is as important as the suggestion itself.

Also, if it failed, I would take responsibility for it and if it succeeded, the team members who contributed were made the heroes of that particular section. That is what being a leader means. If you like taking credit all the time, then your growth will be limited and your own team will phase you out. No one is stronger than all of us.

As a department head, both success and failures make you a winner. You dared to go there, took initiative and tried to solve an issue, that everyone avoided, with enthusiasm and innovative ideas. You are bound to succeed if you are committed and have a motivated team backing you up.

In these situations, when partial results start showing positive signs, my experience tells me that even the other sections—who may not know the intricacies and complexities of the assignment at hand—will come forward to extend their support to see that you succeed.

Success is like an infectious disease. If it is happening in some corner of the organization, others don't want to be left behind. All would like to join the bandwagon and not like to be called laggards. Especially when they see results being demonstrated.

It's the environment for success which you need to create to come out with flying colours, thus chalking your path to move up the hierarchy.

It is generally observed that—after achieving this 'Never Happened Before' type of success—organizations are then set on a different trajectory of growth. It bolsters their confidence to such an extent that everything becomes achievable. They proactively start setting milestones. What we need to take care of is the momentum. One needs many creative and mature line managers with drive and enthusiasm to take it forward and learn from the success of your well-conceived and effectively implemented initiatives. But you are the one that sets the ball rolling if you take that risk. You will always be remembered as such. Take that risk.

Your Plan

Career Stage: Department Head

Promotion Received:

Next Position:

My Timeline:

Challenges I Will Address
- Challenge 1:
- Challenge 2:
- Challenge 3:

Skills I Need to Develop to Take Up the Challenges
- Skill 1:
- Skill 2:
- Skill 3:

Mentors I Can Reach Out to for Each Challenge
- Mentor 1:
- Mentor 2:
- Mentor 3:

8

Building a Strong Network

Career Stage: Multiple Department Head

- **Award Entries**: It's equally important that your performance, the results, your efforts and your keenness to help the organization don't go unnoticed. And nothing shows it better than a shiny trophy in your office
- **Network Beyond the Company**: Have professionals of other divisions, sections and other sister concerns on your friend list
- **Seminars and Events**: Create opportunities to interact with a new network and stay in touch with the old
- **Trust Your Team**: This will be your secret weapon
- **Givers Gain**: Reciprocate their efforts to highlight yourself in a similar way. Give as much as you get
- **Your Plan**

At this level, you are responsible for several departments and each one will make demands on your time. You need to have a game plan to make sure you are not just capable and efficient in your new role, but excel at it.

Award Entries

I wrote a lot in the earlier chapters on how you need to make sure your team is complimented and you find ways of getting your team and your own work noticed. However, when you head several departments, you need to drive this up several notches. It shouldn't be assumed that someone else will take your success story to the higher-ups or to the world. It may finally happen, but I am assuming it would be too late by then.

Awards are a smart and subtle way of drawing attention to your leadership style and work put in by you and your team to the benefit of the organization. Tata Steel had a unique concept to showcase good work and crowdsourcing solutions. They held Annual Quality Improvement Projects, highlighting a team's efforts in a very structured and organized way. All the sections across the organization would list down the burning issues and a team of four to six members was formed under a leader to resolve these issues. All the team members were experienced and had expertise in problem-solving techniques with the help of 7-QC Tools. This was a coveted platform.

The teams would get cracking and, at the end of the year, the completed and audited reports were submitted to the select group of judges to assess the usefulness and their impact on the functioning of the section or division. The best teams were then selected for awards, recognition and public appreciation in a glittering ceremony. The top brass of the organization would be present during this show and the evening would end with a photoshoot, trophies and dinner with the top management. One can imagine the impact on the morale of the team and the concerned section. These winners used to become catalysts of healthy competition and a problem-solving mindset. Every year, all divisions would vie for a place on the stage next to the MD, Dr J.J. Irani/Mr Nerulkar and Mr Muthuraman, over a period of time.

This culture had a lasting impact on raising performance and as a result, customer satisfaction.

I remember that one of my earlier bosses, Suren Rao, would create dedicated teams for enhancing customer satisfaction and aim for 'zero defects'. Many of the senior executives would head these teams and the results were extremely satisfying. We entered the awards with our customers as a supplier for a couple of years and got better each year. Each submission was essential, as was attending the awards ceremony. We got to know more about the winners and what mattered to the judges. The final win did wonders not just for the team, but the overall organization's morale.

I recall that it took us almost six years of continuous participation in JRD QV Awards, a very healthy competition among all companies of the Tata group to showcase their success stories on quality and many other business parameters to reach a stage of success. This platform was extremely useful to bring up a very planned and step-by-step success by involving each and every employee, and all other stakeholders including suppliers, customers and the community around you. Changing the mindset of all and looking at the business from the Tata perspective of doing ethical business took a heavy toll on our resources but the tenacity finally paid off. We were at the dais to receive recognition of our efforts from the group chairman, Ratan Tata, in 2008, and I think it was one of the proudest moments of my career. The whole company felt on top of the world when these achievements were publicly appreciated and recognized.

This was a practice I took to heart and imbibed in my team when I achieved this position. At the start of the year, we would map out one customer satisfaction award that we would like to aim for. Through the year, we put together material and reviewed it consistently to ensure we had a good entry. During my tenure we won many awards, including the Toyota Best Supplier Award, Bajaj Best Supplier Award, and were runners-up in JRD Quality Value Award and TPM Excellence Award by JIPM, Japan; Suren Rao was the mentor in the process of achieving this award. It was an extremely important milestone in the history of Tata Bearings. It was always a surprise for the community when a small division in the Tata community took away the prize. It did not happen overnight. We worked for it every single day, ensuring that we had a good entry. The earlier disappointments of not winning the award were quickly forgotten.

I recall that our MD, Mr Muthuraman, has mentioned in one of the forums to all the executives of Tata Steel to visit my company for benchmarking in quality and productivity excellence. The highest compliment one can expect to get.

Winning awards also got me noticed not just in my organization, but also within the Tata community and beyond. Don't leave this to chance. Plan for it.

The hallmark of survival in our case was the burning desire to be the best and a continuous endeavour to improve ourselves to achieve set goals. The size of the company was small, but small could be beautiful and still be a shining star and excel in many fields, depending on your priorities which meet the customers' and other stakeholders' expectations. We were able to successfully inculcate this burning desire to be competitive as a team and company in all the employees, helping them understand that we were a team. We could not win it alone. The motto which we spread all around, displayed in every nook and corner, printed on T-shirts and other gifts, was *One Team, One Dream*. And the dream was to excel in whatever we did.

When you and your department win an award, don't leave any stone unturned in promoting it. If failure doesn't take much time to be blown out of proportion, then why not success? Leverage your teams and network to promote it. For any grand success, throw a bash at the clubhouse for the department and then carry it forward with more home dinner celebrations involving core teams. These department bashes were well attended by teams, their spouses and vendors. Spouses are equally important. My wife stood by me as we made these rounds and was instrumental in helping women in the community have a positive mindset towards success and failure. We encouraged spouses to celebrate their partners' achievements.

We also took the time to invite not just our seniors and group-level management seniors, but also industry peers from complementary verticals so that the word of mouth carried forward beyond our own circle. At these well-attended bashes, we ensured deserving team members were recognized and awarded with citations.

We now live in a digital age. A digital marketing campaign, including heartfelt stories and posts on social media platforms—that are further amplified by your team ensuring they are noticed by several new networks across designations—is a goldmine. Use it.

Network Beyond the Company

While you might be excellent at your job, you might wonder sometimes why you were overlooked for a promotion or project. You might be the best candidate for the job, but someone more popular got the position. Someone who might not have the same mastery over the technical aspects of your job as you, would have swiped that promotion away from you. You may be surprised when you achieve some milestones that your set goal hasn't materialized. Even though you reached the bus stop, the bus did not arrive or you missed it. It's a heart-breaking and shattering experience. So close and yet so far.

Here is when I ask candidates . . . did you tell someone that you were waiting for the bus? When the bus arrived, did you let the driver know you wanted to get on it? Did you have the currency to buy the bus ticket?

The currency in this case is the network you have, along with a fair dose of accolades and trust that you have found among your networks.

I have experienced this in my career too. You may be the winning horse, but the jockey is highlighted. It's almost the same story, irrespective of the generation we belong to. This is not the time to brood and withdraw yourself into a shell of bitterness and resentment. This is the time you dig in your heels and start working even more aggressively.

Your smart work and consistent result delivery for years together will keep you in the limelight of glory and put you on the high pedestal of recognition. This is the time you move beyond your own peers and company and reach out to create a stronger network at the group and industry levels. Keep in mind that these could be networks of industries that are complementary to your own. They could also be educational. Your alumni are a strong network that you should not miss out on. And awards are a great way to start. When you win, everyone would want to network with you. When you don't, be gracious and seek out the winner to congratulate them. That is another networking opportunity.

Only when you network and swap stories or solutions, do you gain new insights and learnings that could help you solve challenging issues in your own organization.

In the process, you also make some good friends who you can share your thoughts with, without competition. These networks will vouch for your competence, deep knowledge and sincerity for the growth of the organization. It is a win-win situation when you reciprocate the same feelings.

You garner support not only based on your excellent PR skills (which, by the way, is crucial here), but also based on your high level of understanding business complexities.

The top brass generally takes in views from many outsiders too before putting you in the top position, as they would like to know more about your strengths beyond the company. Here, your networking circle comes in very handy to help you build up your image. Nurture these relationships with genuine interest and friendship. It also prepares you to be able to speak to just about anyone. And trust me, this is an art form that takes years of practice.

Many times, I have come across professionals with average IQ, no product and no customer knowledge who would take over as business heads. Their strength: having extremely strong networking skills. Their expertise in people management takes them ahead for some time, but then they get trapped in their own web of incompetency and lack of knowledge of product complexities. Imagine if you had both. While having a sound technical knowledge base will be a strong foundation for you to start with, imagine if you have excellent people skills to sweeten the pot. It will help you reach the top faster.

At this point, as a professional and parent, I would like to mention that in our country, it is unfortunate that most parents continue to push their children to become toppers with high grades. High cut-off percentages set by educational institutions feed the parents' obsession with marks more than children's. This only pushes them into impossible situations and emotions they are unable to deal with. Now, when you read these last couple of chapters, you will understand that while having a sound technical base gives you a great start, it is only your people skills that will get you ahead. Most engineers I know are bad at this and quit the race at a familiar level. Some push through because they want the next position.

Developing your people skills and emotional quotient from a young age will help you at every stage. If you were not given this chance, then ensure you give it your children. Give them a chance to be confident and happy adults. It warms my heart that today all three of my children are confident and successful entrepreneurs in their own fields. In my household, they would be more tense about their marks owing to societal pressure . . . often much more than me. I would always encourage them to put in their best and keep moving forward. Being a part of the extra-curricular activities that developed their confidence was not an easy task, given the societal pressure on being a high scorer instead of a good person. A high score is not the endgame.

Golden rules of networking:
- While you connect with like-minded people, always include a few who have opposing views and challenge you to think.
- Connect with someone who inspires you and can mentor you.
- Stay away from negative people and ROI-driven networkers.
- Don't be needy or desperate.
- Ask them about their story before sharing yours.
- Listen. Don't speak only to respond.

- Be generous and empathetic.
- Be respectful.
- Cross connect to help when you can.
- Be genuine in your support.

Seminars and Events

Networking, we agree, gives you the edge. But where will you network and find like-minded people? Especially since your multi-department responsibilities take so much of your time. Seminars and events are a great place to start. Make time for them, instead of delegating or nominating your team members for all of them.

These are also the places where you gain additional knowledge. Leadership and learning go hand in hand. Never forget that. I have often seen that after a certain position, professionals start falling in love with their designations. They forget that the moment they leave that position, people will forget about them and that to keep that position, they need to continue to upskill and learn.

A lot of companies now give sufficient importance to upskilling. They encourage budding executives and possible future leaders to attend seminars, technical and marketing events in the country as well as abroad. The intent is not only to understand the basic purpose of the programme, but also to build up confidence to meet and share thoughts and ideas with many new people from different countries and develop new contacts. The faster you increase the circle, the better your chances of improving your skills and thus, strengthening your prospects of being an all-rounder who can fit in any known or unknown situation and can come out of it unscathed and successfully.

I made it a point to attend at least one seminar or event every year, with notable speakers, to upskill my knowledge. Professionals at these events have the same agenda and would be at the same position as you. What better place to learn and share ideas? Your ideas and attitude will leave an impression.

Trust Your Team

You move ahead to the next level only if you have a competent team that has your back. When you take over this role, meet the department heads and identify who could be a capable second-in-command. Groom two people from each department and equip them with skills and expertise that will help them do their job efficiently and with sincerity. When they do their job well, it requires less of your time. It leaves you with enough time to think and strategize on how to bring about growth and showcase it. This is equally essential. Help your department heads understand this and take them into confidence. When they know, you are working to showcase their success, their attitude changes to that of support and gratitude. You need to be courageous and take the first step to trust them.

Givers Gain

The more you give, the more you gain. This is a long-term investment that might or might not give you the gains you planned for but will give you the gains you need. When you network, learn and mentor your team . . . be free with knowledge and support. Be genuine when you do that.

At this stage in my career, at the age of seventy-three, I am still experiencing givers' gain. All my networks, even at this stage of life, are still in touch with me. Youngsters ask for advice for growth or a career crisis and senior members talk shop, and seek and support me on the personal front. I call it a lifelong win-win situation.

Here is where I must caution you: take up only as much as you can handle. The more you help, the more warmth builds up in the cockles of your heart. It can get addictive. However, taking up a job and doing it badly will only have negative ripple effects in your network. If you cannot make the time for it, direct them to someone who has the time to help them. Don't take it up and not do it.

Your Plan

Career Stage: Multiple Department Head

Promotion Received:

Next Position:

My Timeline:

Award Entries
Awards I will enter this year:
- Award 1:
- Award 2:
- Award 3:

Network Beyond the Company
What I can make time for this year:
- Network 1:
- Network 2:
- Network 3:

Seminars and Events
Must attend:
- Event 1:
- Event 2:
- Event 3:

Team Lead

Will help these professionals be better leaders:
- Department 1:
- Department 2:
- Department 3:

Givers Gain

Three people I intend to help unconditionally
- Individual 1:
- Individual 2:
- Individual 3:

9

Create an Opening for Yourself

Career Stage: No. 2 in the Organization/Vice President

- **Breaking the Mould**: In most well-performing organizations, the organization structure, once set, does not get amended for a long time. But if you are to set yourself apart from the rest of the pack, then learn to break the mould and create a completely new one
- **The Inner Circle**: The friends you have will determine the pace of your success
- **Paving a Path Ahead**: Be generous with ideas to the people who matter. Become their 'idea'/go-to person
- **Your Plan**

Breaking the Mould

When you climb up the ladder, the positions thin out as do the opportunities. You will find it harder and harder to push through and break the ranks.

When you are on the last lap, you will often come across situations where you will stop growing in the hierarchy. The feeling of 'being stuck' in your career becomes prevalent as do the 'no opening' messages being conveyed across verticals. It is a frustrating situation to handle, go through and share. In an organization which has stopped growing in any direction, this problem becomes more serious. Many HR exit surveys reveal the lack of growth opportunities as one of the top reasons why employees quit an organization and try out somewhere else. But quitting doesn't ensure that you are heading for greener pastures or that you are bound to reach your desired goal if you jump ship.

Every organization has its own way of working and nothing is assured by any management when it comes to the top post. Your career path will be charted till the No. 2 level at the organization at the max. Beyond that, there are no guarantees.

It happened with me too. I missed the opportunity to a rank newcomer from another division of the big organization. While I thought that I was the most suitable candidate to take over, I was surprised and hurt that my candidacy was not considered. When I met the decision makers and spoke to them about this and about my prospects for the future, I was met with a blunt refusal in no uncertain words. What was conveyed to me was: take it or leave it.

This was one of the toughest situations that I had to go through. Being so close to the top and yet not being allowed in or given a seat at the table.

But there had to be a way out.

The first option could be to move out and look at a parallel or upskilled position. The second option could be to put your nose to the grind and push through for a new position. I chose the latter.

Keep working wherever you are with new zeal for the betterment of the organization. It calls for true grit and strength of a person's character to continue at the same place. This, with a positive attitude and a futuristic view. Quitting with a hurt ego and bitterness may seem like an easy thing to do, but it comes with its own risks and hurdles. Also keep in mind that at this position, jobs are hard to come by.

Be a fighter and keep the challenger spirit alive. Keep demonstrating your expertise and resilience. Grab new challenging assignments, work beyond your defined boundary of work and participate with decision makers to take the company ahead. Make your presence felt. It not only revives your spirits, but also enhances your esteem in the eyes of the top management as you continue to exhibit your tenacity and zeal to work.

At this point, I came across an interesting challenge. The biggest buyer of our company's product had started lodging several complaints with our marketing executives about unsatisfactory product performance and service. It was decided that a task force was to be created, with me heading it, along with two other senior executives. We were to address this issue and solve it.

I took my task force to the customers' factory and camped there for a few days. We worked with them to understand the challenge, discussed the issue and provided tweaks on the spot that would not hold up their manufacturing. This also gave us a chance to arrive at a few possible options and get them approved on the spot to the customer's satisfaction.

The customer liked the determined approach as we were keen to eliminate the problematic situation. With a few trials and repeat visits on the shop floor, we had a delighted customer whose loyalty and admiration we won with our earnestness and intent. This left a big imprint on the customer satisfaction process of our company, which was horizontally deployed to many other customers too. This was the type of challenge where any mishap or failure could have put the survival of the business as well as my own personal ambitions in jeopardy.

This crucial success also left an imprint on the minds of the concerned people in my own company about my capabilities and resilience. This attitude helped me migrate from the have-nots zone to the haves zone and re-establish my place in the running.

The Inner Circle

At this juncture, you will feel the acute need for sound professional advice from your inner circle that could have possibly avoided this heart-breaking moment. These are typical HR issues and closely linked with many inside developments taking place at a certain level. As a person who is totally engrossed in delivering results irrespective of the odds, this parameter could escape your notice as it did mine.

Creating a tight-knit inner circle and drawing it in further is essential at this point. A close colleague from other sister organizations, ex-colleagues familiar with behind-the-scenes developments, mentors and a close confidant in your company should be members of your inner circle. Each one will help you overcome this challenge with a fresh perspective. The inner circle should comprise of successful executives with a positive mindset who have already accomplished their goal and can look beyond their own needs to help someone else. In this circle of relationships, do not let any inhibitions hold you back. Talk your heart out and seek advice.

Positive vibes and mindset are essential for the inner circle. Positivity itself brings miracles in our behaviour and helps us get strong mental as well as physical strength to surmount all odds.

Start young when you start developing your inner circle. Through my school and college years, I befriended my own batchmates and seniors as well. Slowly, this circle grew to include more seniors and a few peers more experienced and knowledgeable in the field where I had just made an entry. I took the chance to learn from them. This is how you start. Learning the knack of creating a close inner circle will benefit you throughout your career.

Paving a Path Ahead

When life throws you a curveball, yell 'plot twist' at the top of your lungs and carry on. We all have an ideal view of what our lives should look like. Unfortunately, not everything goes the way you want it to. It would be unwise to assume it will. Unrealistic expectations will lead to bigger heartaches and even bigger disappointments. On this last lap to the top spot, dig your heels in, instead of packing up. Packing up and trying out somewhere else is the last option and one of the most difficult to achieve at this stage in your career. And it's easier said than done, as openings at the top of the ladder are few and not immediately available. Bite back those sharp retorts and keep working to find a possible re-route. Your new boss could be the well-wisher you were missing and could be the person who would give you the opportunity to move ahead to the next round.

In my case, I happened to get a person with high empathy and an unbiased professional outlook, who helped me rebuild my career path. He was instrumental in my growth towards the top spot. Always remember, you can never go ahead if you work alone. No one owes you anything . . . especially not the company you work in. Your talent and loyalty will get you only so far. Only with the support of well-wishers who see the talent in you, can you cross the last hurdle.

If you opt to move out of the company at this juncture, then make sure the company you are moving to has offered you what you want and charted a career path for you for the next ten years. Without this, it is pointless. You will end up disappointed there as well and will be starting from scratch.

I would advise that you opt for continuation. But the efforts to make your presence felt have to be increased because next time, there should be no chance of failure and disappointment.

Now, if you decide to stay, like me, look at sinking your teeth into bigger challenges that threaten the existence or operation of the company and could blast the hurdles and pave a path for you to the next stop.

In my organization, we were expanding production capacity and looking for manufacturing equipment that would help us achieve that. With due diligence and other inputs, we negotiated and decided to pick up a well-established manufacturing unit (not utilized properly). The management tasked me with the entire operation that would require making the massive shift of huge infrastructure to our manufacturing base, commissioning it and getting it inaugurated on a fixed date. This was a challenge worth taking to prove my mettle. With a handpicked team and support of the top brass, the mission was accomplished with a few days to spare. It was a brilliant way to stay in the reckoning for the top position at the next opportunity. And it worked.

Don't sit idle and wait for the opportunity to knock at your door. Create it, grab it and accomplish it. Every organization, small or big, has multiple challenges at any given point. Identify the ones that could be potential disasters or are proceeding to be, highlight and sell your idea with its implementation plan and the benefits the organization is going to accrue.

Keep exhibiting a positive attitude and lend a helping hand, as always. Maintain your style of working. While you do this, continue your own personal campaign for the top position. Keep meeting decision makers formally or informally and stay in the race. You may be given some feedback: act on it. Keep sharing your vision to manage the business and your contributions so far.

Keeping creativity alive is also essential. I have observed in my career span that creative executives who have the knack to think outside the box continue to be at the forefront of recognition and rewards. This behavioural aspect is the winning trait of those successful executives who could fulfil and achieve their life's goal. When you are at this crucial juncture, don't box that thinking in. This is the time to get the creative juices flowing and add more to the mix.

This is one of those hard tasks that could require a strategic shift in thinking and how you approach it. Self-counseling and self-talk help in maintaining mental resilience and strength. Believing in your own self is crucial at this point. You are your biggest supporter, so you cannot let negative talk bog you down.

The fire in the belly to reach the top post should never be allowed to get extinguished till the last lap of the race. The difference between the victor and also-ran is always the last mile. Are you willing to invest and push yourself during the last mile to reach it?

Your Plan

Career Stage: No. 2 in the organization/vice president

Promotion Received:

Next Position:

My Timeline:

Breaking the Mould
Changes I will bring at this position:
- Department: Change:
- Department: Change:
- Department: Change:

The Inner Circle
Professionals in my inner circle at this stage:
- Mentor:
- Ex-Boss:
- Colleague:
- Industry Peer:

Paving a Path Ahead
Challenges I will leverage to create an opening:
- Challenge 1:
- Challenge 2:
- Challenge 3:

10

Keep Marketing Yourself for the Top Job

Career Stage: One Step to the Boardroom

- **Handling Failure at the Top**: Every role will bring a new challenge and you might not be able to win all of them
- **Cut the Fluff**: Be a straight-shooter
- **It's Always Day 1**: Bring your A-game to the table. Every. Single. Day.
- **Be Kind**: It will always come back to you in the most unexpected ways
- **Maintain Discipline**: Will hold you in good stead at every position
- **Articulating Your Vision**: Your communication skills matter
- **Letting Go**: There is no other way to move ahead
- **Love**: Are you in it?

- **Family**: They bind you to what matters
- **Your Inner Circle**: Will keep you grounded
- **The Golden Nuggets**: HR and PR
- **Gratitude**: Live it every day
- **Your Plan**

Getting to the top is a long marathon that you will invest in throughout your career. Staying there is a whole different ballgame. You might be there for a couple of years or a decade. Whatever the duration of your stint, aim to leave a positive impression and hand it over to your successor as an improved version. During my stint at the top, these were the major challenges I faced, and I would share these with you in this chapter. As you read this, you will realize that the trappings are all human relationships and not technical in nature. Know the signs, learn to recognize the pattern and catch them to change them before they take hold of you.

Handling Failure at the Top

It's well understood that there are going to be instances of failure at every level of hierarchy, be it at the middle-management level or the top-management level. Mark my words, you will also make them at the top. The only difference is that, at this position, all eyes and the spotlight will be on you. Every step you take will leave a significant footprint. You don't have anyone shielding you from the top and being the shield. You are the shield. Maintaining a proper balance of failure and success is an important trait of a mature and capable person that will be expected of you when you are at the top. How you handle both will determine your next year, review or posting. Your team will look towards you for direction and will implement it as an acceptable way of behaviour across the company.

It's important to talk about failure at the top level and I will do that because no one else will. Your attitude and the strength of your mental fortitude will determine how quickly you can rectify or turn around the situation. I personally believe failures make a person stronger, determined and keep their feet firmly on the ground. At the top, you need to take a calculated risk and do a risk analysis of the situation before you take it up.

When you succeed, celebrate with the whole team. When you fail, do an analysis before speaking, so you can adjust your responses accordingly. Don't . . . rather never pick on a single team member in a public forum to pin the blame on. Brandishing a scapegoat on a public forum is never a sign of good leadership. Having said that, if you spot crucial mistakes made by an individual or a team that sank the boat, bring them into your office and have a personal chat with them.

Cut the Fluff

You are the person who has to be the straight talker. If you mean or promise something . . . then do it. When it comes to taking risks, lay the cards on the table for your team and seniors or other board members very clearly. Altercations and heartaches happen when unrealistic expectations are set. These will set you up for failure. Do not oversell.

It's Always Day 1

Keep that fire burning and bring it with you every day. Start every day like the first day of the appointment . . . with the same zeal, dedication and enthusiasm. Because you got the job does not mean you can sit back and relax. Keep the fire of ambition burning. It will urge you to move ahead and propel yourself forward. There will be other contenders and usurpers. You need to earn your place at the top, every single day. Occupying the top job is not the most comfortable chair to sit in and relax. It marks the beginning of a new phase of one's career where you need to look ahead and put your mind to solving the challenges of the company that will bring in new heights of performance, results and recognition. And it calls for more work, more than you have ever done in your career so far.

Be Kind

When you get chosen for the top position, there would be others who you would have competed with. However much you think you are the right and the most deserving candidate for the job, others will also think the same. These will be friends and peers you have worked with, went out for picnics with and whose families you have bonded with. There are a couple of outcomes that could take place.

Some will resent you and quit, some will accept the decision and work with you, others will gracefully bow out of the race altogether and move out. Either way, it is your job to address this head on. For the first category: a straight chat works, and they will take any of the other two routes. If they do, it works for you. For the second category: you have a friend in them and should put them in key positions that they can continue to prove themselves in. These will also be great successors that you can groom. For the third: be the large-hearted person who acknowledges their contributions and gives them a heartwarming farewell. Do the same for their spouses as well, however difficult it might be. They will come around eventually.

Maintain your dignity and never plead for someone to accept you, reason with them for your position, defend your promotion or beseech them to stay with you. It will never happen and will only serve to bring you down in their eyes and your own.

Maintain Discipline

This is the time a lot of peers and friends will expect favours. It is a dangerous sinkhole. Most, at this point, start handing them out in the interest of keeping the team together. That is a perilous road to go down on. This is where the earlier discipline you maintained about meritocracy will work in your favour. You would have worked with most of the team and know their strengths and weaknesses. Create the team that will help you win. Do this with kindness but with a good dose of firmness. Your critical reviews, PERT chart monitoring and walk-the-talk style will hold you in good stead here and whatever level you may have been operating on.

Articulate Your Vision

Any successful company spends lots of resources on brand building and sharing its future plans with all stakeholders. But these are the unending journeys that one takes up to stay in the market and earn profits.

Smart companies would like to stay ahead of their competitors. And the only way to do that is to look into the future and articulate a new strategy, a new vision and a new way to handle future expectations. Sharing of the vision with all in the chain is of utmost importance and helps you to march ahead to achieve it. A feeling of shared vision has to be generated in every person starting from suppliers to the last person in the process. This will bring your communication skills in sharp focus.

You must define the vision in a simple and easily understandable language for all. Once you master this, it becomes easy for anyone to comprehend, from the MD to a security watchman. Avoid complications and adopt the simple technique of Keep It Simple Silly (KISS) when drafting communication.

Your own vision, which you have been envisaging for so many years, needs to be discussed, shared with and articulated by your top team. Refine it with their inputs and make it a shared vision that will set the direction and the path your company will take in the next few years. It calls for total participation by one and all, including you . . . especially you. You are the leader who will make it happen. Roll up your sleeves and get cracking. Walk the talk.

Letting Go

Just let it go: All the pettiness and vindication and animosity with past, present and future colleagues, juniors, seniors. It will not do you any good to dwell on it. I have seen, in my career, top bosses waste their energy and time on finding fault and digging into old files to find out what wrongs were committed by their predecessors. I can assure you that these not-so-gentlemen were on the downhill journey from the day they occupied that top chair. Don't indulge in this petty self-destructive activity. These individuals lose respect of all their peers and juniors as this erstwhile vindictive nature spills over on to everyday work. And it will spill over.

Looking towards the future and creating a vision of excellence is the hallmark of a true leader. They are remembered and appreciated by latter generations and successors who are going to manage the show within the framework of values and professional ethics laid down by their illustrious predecessors. Be one of them.

Love

Don't fall in love with your designation or chair. You are here for the job. Do it to the best of your ability. Create relationships that are genuine and will last beyond the chair. One of the biggest mistakes most of us make is that we are not able to distinguish between the genuine love showered on us and our Chair, which we happen to occupy at that point. Disappointment will set in if you expect the majority of the people to still treat you as they did when you were the boss. Understand that this is human nature and there is nothing you can do to change it. Focus on collecting relationships that will outlast the job. And don't fall in love with the chair.

Family

They bind you to what matters in life. This position will have a lot of demands on your time. Don't let what is really important in life slip through because of it. It will strain all your personal relationships with family. Your spouse and you need to have a firm understanding on how to manage the home team. This is the team that will truly celebrate you. Once you move on from this position, these are the relationships that will continue forever. For want of a battle, don't lose the war.

Your Inner Circle

At this stage, your inner circle will get sifted and be left with a few handfuls. Draw them in closer. This is the circle that will keep you grounded and also be your strength. Be mindful about who you include in this inner circle. This is yours and yours alone. These are the people who have stayed with you through thick and thin. Keep them close to you.

The Golden Nuggets: HR and PR

Growing up, you must have been often told to let go of sports, arts or extra-curricular activities to focus on studies. Now you understand that the things that set you apart cannot be found in books. It is only by interacting with people that you are able to ground your humanity, interact with the public and develop strong relationships and bonds that will last you a lifetime. Knowing how to handle and interact with people is one of the strongest suits that will keep you moving ahead in life. If you are lucky to be reading this in the formative years of your career, then start now. If not . . . then start now. It is never too late to learn these skills.

Gratitude

True leaders will always exhibit this key quality. Gratitude towards colleagues, peers, seniors, juniors and mentors is a humble and endearing trait. However, temper this with discipline. Expressing gratitude does not mean you will bend over backwards for someone. It means you are thankful and will do everything in your power to help set things right. It will also mean you will not shy away from acknowledging their contribution towards your career. You might not always be in a position to grant them favours but will always remember and genuinely thank them with a sincere intention to help. That is what it meant for me. You can choose to define it any way you want.

My experience of life has made me realize that the habit of expressing gratitude is one of the most heartwarming ways of living with an easy conscience. When your heart is light, you will be more genuine and sincere which will shine though.

In this whole exercise of projecting yourself for the top job is a good human being. When you are sitting at the top, you will be expected to deliver results against which you will be judged at the end of the year, but a humane approach is in your hands.

My golden rule in life has always been to see the good in situations and have a humane approach. Just because someone else is bad does not mean that you stop being good. Hold your head higher. Vibrate at a higher frequency. Take the first step to reach the last step of the ladder. Enjoy the journey of Excellence and Success!

Your Plan

Day 1: Create a Legend

Ten Golden Rules: In the Boardroom

Print and paste this on your soft board on your first day

- Don't be petty or vindictive
- Take up a meritocratic approach
- Reprimand in private and praise in public
- Keep your word
- Your communication skills matter
- Lead by example
- Don't let success or failure get to you
- Express gratitude and maintain a positive attitude
- Discipline is essential to your success
- Celebrate all victories

Acknowledgements

I convey my heartiest thanks to my daughter Tarunjeet, who helped me throughout the journey of writing with her invaluable tips to refine and express my thought process in the form of this book.

In the nearly fifty years of my life in the corporate world and academia, there have been many subordinates, peers and seniors who have supported and guided me. Some of them, to whom I convey my thanks, are: Dr J.J. Irani, B. Muthuraman, Dr T. Mukherjee, S.L. Deoras, Harsh Jha and Suren Rao. They contributed immensely with their rich experience, which helped me to take the right decisions.

I am extremely thankful to my colleagues and friends A. Chaudhury, K.N. Rao, Dipankar Ghosh, Bidyut Ghosh, Shyamal Sinha, J.S. Shastry, Rakesh Chandra, J.V.R. Sarma, Renu Arora and Dr Jyoti Kaul Mattoo, who supported me at the crucial junctions of my journey with their competent advice.

A big thank you to my daughters Harminder and Sahiba, who kept motivating me.

And lastly, I would like to thank my wife, Verjeet, for extending unconditional support and inspiring me during the writing of this book. I wish she was here with us to see the launch of *Ten Steps to the Boardroom*.